EXISTENCE, RELATEDNESS, AND GROWTH

EXISTENCE, RELATEDNESS, AND GROWTH

Human Needs in Organizational Settings

Clayton P. Alderfer

Fp
The Free Press, New York
Collier–Macmillan Limited, London

The Free Press
A Division of The Macmillan Company
866 Third Avenue, New York, New York 10022

Collier-Macmillan Canada Ltd., Toronto, Ontario

Library of Congress Catalog Card Number: 79-148542

Printing number 1 2 3 4 5 6 7 8 9 10

For my parents Ruth and Paul

CONTENTS

Contents

ACKNOWLEDGMENTS

THE work reported in this book began in the mid 1960s when I was just settling into the career of becoming an applied behavioral scientist. From then until now, I have had the good fortune of being supported and stimulated by many people, some of whom I shall be able to mention. It is a pleasure for me to express my appreciation.

Charleen Alderfer helped in about every way that a wife can: by being a research assistant, an editor, a critic, and a patient, honest, and joyful companion. More than any single person, Chris Argyris influenced my entry into this field, and over the years has been very helpful to me in aiding my entry into organizations and in commenting on my work. My intellectual debt to Abraham Maslow will be very apparent to anyone who reads beyond the first chapter. He saw a first draft of this manuscript and offered his comments. I regret he will not see the final version. Jean Miller was my very committed and effective secretary.

Many colleagues have offered their constructive criticism of earlier versions of parts or all of this work, and I wish to thank them (knowing that I shall probably miss some): Thomas Lodahl, Vernon Buck, Edward Lawler, Tim Hall, Richard Hackman, Benjamin Schneider, Fritz Steele, Warren Bennis, Donald Taylor, Martin Evans, Gerritt Wolf, Lee Bolman, Harvey Wagner, and Mark Sandberg.

The many respondents who gave willingly of their time and effort cannot be named in order to protect the confidentiality of the participating organizations. I thank them anonymously for what they gave and for their part in what I learned.

Clayton P. Alderfer
New Haven, Connecticut

Special acknowledgment is offered for the following:

The last quotation on p. 21 is reprinted with permission of The Institute for Social Research, The University of Michigan, from Nancy C. Morse, *Satisfactions in the White Collar Job*. Ann Arbor: Institute for Social Research, 1953.

The quotation on p. 34 is reprinted with permission from Samuel Gompers, *Labor and the Common Welfare*. New York: E. P. Dutton. Copyright 1920 by E. P. Dutton and Co., Inc., publishers.

The questions on pp. 157-159 are reprinted by permission of Holt, Rinehart and Winston, Inc. from Chapter One, "The Assessment of Human Motives" by Gardner Lindzey, from *Assessment of Human Motives* edited by Gardner Lindzey. Copyright © 1958 by Gardner Lindzey.

Table 5.2, p. 78, is reprinted by permission of the American Psychological Association from Clinton Alderfer, "Convergent and discriminant validation of satisfaction and desire measures by interviews and questionnaires," *Journal of Applied Psychology*, 1967, *51*, page 514, Table 4.

The quotations on pp. 26 and 27 are reprinted by permission of the American Psychological Association from A. H. Maslow, "A theory of human motivation," *Psychological Review*, 1943, *50*, p. 386.

Chapter 1

INTRODUCTION

L ong before behavioral science developed in the twentieth century, social philosophers, theologians, and thoughtful men of many disciplines asked themselves about the nature of man. What were his primary wishes, his most fundamental needs? What motivated the human animal? The answers to these questions rarely showed agreement. Even the way the questions were posed changed from person to person, from generation to generation, and from century to century. Even today behavioral science, while an accepted field of study, has not (as yet) provided a clear consensus of answers to these questions.

The present study is concerned with human needs in the form of of the desires and satisfactions that people experience as they participate in organizational life. Two basic questions form the central themes of the work. First, how do a person's satisfactions relate to his desires? Second, how do a person's desires relate to his tendency to obtain satisfaction? Together these questions rest on the working assumptions that a person's desires are in part determined by his perceptions of the returns he obtains from his external world and that his desires in part also determine the nature of the returns he is able to perceive from his external world.

The search for answers to these questions and for tests of the underlying assumptions was carried out through a series of empirical studies in organizational settings. Early in the research, I attempted to formulate some theoretical concepts and explanatory mechanisms. In developing the concepts, I was heavily influenced by

Abraham Maslow's (1954) theory of human motivation. At the same time, however, the beginning was also a time to develop methods for collecting empirical data so that one could more readily find support, disconfirmation, or a basis for revising theoretical ideas.

OVERVIEW

Existence, relatedness, and growth (E.R.G.) theory is the name of the conceptual product that has resulted from these investigations. Existence, relatedness, and growth are the basic categories used to conceptualize human needs and will be defined in Chapter 2. Maslow's theory of human motivation has provided a number of concepts which have been highly influential in the thinking of investigators who have concerned themselves with human motivation in organizational settings. In one sense, the present work carries forward some of the key ideas that Maslow presented. In another sense, the point of view to be presented here is an alternative to Maslow's theory. Perhaps Maslow's major impact has come from his development and elaboration of self-actualization as a fundamental human need and from his proposal that human needs can be ordered according to their prepotency. These two ideas play an important role in the newer model to be presented here. However, there are also major differences between the theories. When one asks about the major categories of human needs, how the needs may be most fruitfully defined, what the impact of frustration is, and how fixed the hierarchy is, then the answers provided by Maslow tend to be different from those offered by the newer model.

A tension between parsimony and comprehensiveness plagues most theoretical efforts. On the one hand, one would prefer to use as few concepts and assumptions as possible to explain the phenomena under study. On the other hand, one would also like to account for as much of the phenomena as possible. It usually takes additional assumptions to expand the scope of a conceptual framework, and, thus, one gives up some parsimony to achieve added scope. The search for a middle-range theory about human needs faces this same dilemma. The case for E.R.G. theory, therefore, rests not only on comparing it to Maslow's work, but also in comparing it to much less complex ways of dealing with human satisfactions and desires. Chapter 2 will also attempt to spell out these comparisons and their implications.

The utility of any theory turns in part on the degree to which it can provide new insights into already existing empirical data. Incongruities and convergences among existing findings also provide stimuli for the formulation of new viewpoints. The purpose of Chapter 3 is to examine relevant studies, other than those done by this investigator, to see how they relate to E.R.G. theory. To the extent that these findings point toward the reformulation of need concepts, the case for modifying current concepts is made stronger. To the degree that the results are consistent with the newer concepts, support for this approach is strengthened.

A number of key methodological decisions governed the nature of the data collected in this investigation. First, there was the choice to operate in *field* settings. To get a real sense of human satisfactions and desires, it seemed best to go where related events happened naturally. But not just any field settings were appropriate for this series of studies. It was important to have settings that differed from each other in ways that related to major theoretical issues. Second, there was the choice to gather data by means of *interviews* and *questionnaires*. These frequently used methods were especially suited for getting data about the subjective states of satisfaction and desire. Measurement development began with the use of interviews, but most of the data reported utilized questionnaires. Third, the results reported here were all *correlational* in the broad sense of that term (Cronbach, 1957). There were no attempts to introduce experimental manipulations in order to create specified states of independent variables. Both static and time-series data were collected, though not all aspects of the theory were tested using dynamic data. As a result questions about causal direction were addressed but not answered with the precision offered by experiments. Fourth, all of the data reported here were obtained through collaborative relations with the organizations studied. In each setting, we agreed that the study would be devoted to the joint goals of adding to knowledge about human motivation and providing diagnostic information about the human system. Chapter 4 presents an account of the organizations that were studied and the reason for their selection. It also includes a description of the instruments employed and the rationale for their design.

To test predictions from a theoretical framework requires the development of measures which make the link between the theoretical concepts and empirical reality. Chapter 5 is devoted to presenting results which bear on the empirical validity of E.R.G. and related concepts. If the conceptualization is useful, then several attempts to measure the same concepts should converge with each other and diverge from measures of other concepts. The measures should also show understandable (perhaps predictable) relations to concepts outside the scope of need theory but complementary to it. The degree of empirical validity found for the measures sets some kind of lower limit for the support one can expect to find for more precise derivations from the theory. It also provides a frame of reference for dealing with questions about the effect of methodological artifacts on the findings.

Chapters 6 to 8 contain the main body of data for testing predictions derived from E.R.G. theory. Each chapter contains the results pertaining to the particular desires contained in its title. One part of a chapter deals with data bearing on propositions which relate satisfaction to desire, while the other part deals with findings on how desires relate to satisfaction. At this point, the construct validity of the theory is being addressed. Chapter 9 then serves as an overview to assess how far we have come and to point toward new directions for further study.

OBJECTIVES

There are several approaches one might employ in viewing this book. For me, each represents part of the picture. Together they characterize my objectives in doing the work. Conceptually, it gives a new theoretical orientation, building on Maslow's and others' conceptualizations. From this perspective my aim is to sharpen, enlarge, and enrich need theory. This approach assumes that need theory can play a part in understanding human motivation and offers E.R.G. theory as a potential improvement over existing need theories.

Empirically, it provides a format for comparing and testing

alternative theoretical views. None of the comparisons is a crucial experiment in the precise sense of that term. However, at various points the empirical consequences of different theoretical orientations can be observed. One can get a sense of where the different theories are adequate, where they are not, and whether there are reasons for preferring one over others. While the two preceding points represent some relatively advanced goals of social science, there is also a sense in which this work is very much a beginning attempt to explore the major research questions in a systematic way. My primary goals are to enlarge the number of questions that investigators ask about human needs and to increase the ways they choose to answer them. There has been very little testing of Maslow's theory, even though it has had a very large influence on both scholars and practitioners in the field of organizational behavior. Many of the concepts that we have about human needs stem from either animal studies, where the generality of the results is open to question, or from clinical case material where the validity of the data is often viewed skeptically.

As subject matter, the material presented here stands at a cross roads of two traditions in the study of organizational behavior. On one side, there is the clinical-organic orientation which tends to utilize need theory for understanding human motivation and for guiding efforts to affect change. This group has shown relatively less interest in collecting systematic data than in developing theoretical concepts. Investigators such as McGregor (1960), Argyris (1964), and Schein (1965) represent the clinical-organic tradition. On the other side, there is the individual differences-psychological measurement tradition which tends to place heavy emphasis on the collection and analysis of systematic empirical data. Investigators from this tradition tend to be less interested in need theory than in other theories, although they sometimes utilize need concepts to enlarge upon older methods of predicting job performance and satisfaction. Researchers such as Porter (1962; 1963), Vroom (1964), and Dunnette (1966) represent this tradition. What I hope is apparent from this introduction is that the present work attempts to participate in both traditions and to speak to both groups.

Chapter 2

THEORY

T HE purpose of this chapter is to present E.R.G. theory and show how it is similar to and different from related viewpoints.

The theory deals primarily with two classes of variables—satisfactions and desires. It postulates three basic need categories which provide the basis for enumerating specific satisfactions and desires. It contains propositions which predict how satisfaction relates to desire, and it deals with the question of how chronic desires relate to satisfaction.[1]

E.R.G. THEORY

Basic Concepts

The definition of terms such as "need," "drive," "instinct," and "motive" has been a point of controversy for some time among students of motivation. Some have actively advocated the abandonment of some or all of such terms (Cohen, A., 1966). Others have avoided a firm position in the discussion (Vroom, 1964). And still others have continued to struggle with the numerous conceptual problems associated with the terms (Etzioni, 1968; Porter and Lawler, 1968). For the purposes of presenting E.R.G. theory, a number of distinctions should be made so that the scope and purpose of the theory can be clarified.

[1] This chapter is a revision of the theoretical portion of "An Empirical Test of a New Theory of Human Needs," *Organizational Behavior and Human Performance,* Vol. 4, No. 2 (May, 1969), by C. Alderfer. © Academic Press.

A common distinction used by those who are willing to utilize need-like concepts is that between primary and secondary motives (Cohen, J., 1970). Primary needs refer to innate tendencies which an organism possesses by the nature of being the type of creature it is. Sometimes this distinction also includes the notion that primary needs are biologically or physiologically rooted. E.R.G. theory holds the view that existence, relatedness, and growth needs are primary needs in the sense of their being innate, but holds open the question of whether all three are biologically based. Secondary needs refer to acquired or learned tendencies to respond. E.R.G. needs can be increased in strength by learning processes but they do not come into being as a result of learning.

E.R.G. is *not* intended to be a theory to explain how people learn, make choices, or perform. It is a theory about the subjective states of satisfaction and desire. Campbell, Dunnette, Lawler, and Weick (1970) have made a useful distinction between two types of motivation theory. One type they term "mechanical" or "process" theories, while the other type is called "substantive" or "content" theories. The first type attempts to define major classes of variables that are important for explaining motivated behavior. The second type are more concerned with what it is within an individual or his environment that energizes and sustains behavior. E.R.G. theory is a content theory.

Although both satisfaction and desire are subjective states of a person, they differ in the degree of subjectivity. Satisfaction concerns the outcome of an event between a person and his environment. It refers to the internal state of a person who has obtained what he was seeking and is synonymous with getting and fulfilling. Because satisfaction involves interaction with a person's environment, its assessment (for both the person and a researcher) hinges in part on the objective nature of a person's external world. Satisfaction depends both upon the way the world "actually" is and how this reality is perceived by the person.

Frustration is the opposite condition from satisfaction. For some operational purposes, one might wish to distinguish between satisfaction and frustration. If one produced an experimental manipulation which attempted to *increase* the gratification of subjects he would call this satisfaction, but if he attempted to *decrease* the gratification of subjects he would call this frustration. A similar point has been made by Rosenzweig (1944), who made a distinction between primary and secondary frustration. In his view, "primary frustration involves the sheer existence of an active need. . . . Secondary frustration more strictly embraces the definition given above, emphasis being placed upon supervenient obstacles or obstructions in the path of the active need."

Compared to satisfaction, desire is even more subjective, for it does not have a necessary external referent. The term refers exclusively to an internal state of a person which may be synonymous with concepts, such as want, preference, need strength, need intensity, and motive. There is no necessary parallel external state for a desire as there is for a satisfaction. Consequently measurement of desires is more difficult. A person may have defenses which prohibit his own awareness of his desires. Even if he is aware of his desires, he may not choose to report them because he doubts if he would benefit from doing so. Fundamentally, a person is alone with his desires. He cannot rely on a shared consensus of social reality to find out what he wants.

A further distinction may be made between *episodic* and *chronic* desires. *Episodic* desires tend to be situation specific, and they change in response to relevant changes in the situation. Statements about episodic changes in desires are intended to apply across people, without regard for individual differences. *Chronic* desires, on the other hand, reflect more or less enduring states of a person. They are seen as being a consequence both of episodic desires and of learning. To partial out the effects of chronic and episodic desires would require a study which, to some degree, was longitudinal.

According to this definitional system, the term "need" is a concept subsuming both desires and satisfactions (frustrations). For example, when a statement contains the words "existence needs," it includes both existence desires and existence satisfactions (frustrations). Depending on one's theory, there may be no reason to distinguish between the terms "desire," "satisfaction," and "need." If there were always a correspondence between lack of satisfaction (or frustration) and desire, one might abandon these terms and simply refer to "need" as the presence of a deficiency or excess which, if not altered, would impair the health of the organism (Hall, 1961, pp. 30 ff.). This view stems from the Hullian drive theory and will be discussed below under the subject of "the simple frustration hypothesis," one alternative view to E.R.G. theory.

In recent years, there has been an increasing tendency to make use of open-systems concepts for understanding the human personality (Allport, 1960, 1961; von Bertalanffy, 1968). This approach offers the possibility of bridging the gap between those views of man which tend to view him primarily in reactive, tension-producing ways and those orientations which tend to focus on his proactive, stimulus-seeking qualities. Acting as a metatheory or broader framework, open-systems theory stands behind E.R.G. theory. All the major concepts and propositions of E.R.G. should be consistent with the logic of open-systems theory. In a loose sense, E.R.G. theory is derived from an open-systems view of man.

The primary categories of human needs follow from the criteria of personality as an open system outlined by Allport (1960, 1961). Existence needs reflect a person's requirement for material and energy exchange and for the need to reach and maintain a homeostatic equilibrium with regard to the provision of certain material substances. Relatedness needs acknowledge that a person is not a self-contained unit but must engage in transactions with his human environment. Growth needs emerge from the tendency of open systems to increase in internal order and differentiation over time as a consequence of going beyond steady states and interacting with the environment.

Existence needs include all the various forms of material and physiological desires. Hunger and thirst represent deficiencies in existence needs. Pay, fringe benefits, and physical working conditions are other types of existence needs. One of the basic characteristics of existence needs is that they can be divided among people in such a way that one person's gain is another's loss when resources are limited. If two people are hungry, for example, the food eaten by one is not available to the other. When a salary decision is made that provides one person or group of people with more pay, it eliminates the possibility of some other person or group getting extra money. This property of existence needs frequently means that a person's (or group's) satisfaction, beyond a bare minimum, depends upon the comparison of what he gets with what others get in the same situation.

However, this comparison is not "interpersonal" in the sense of necessitating comparison with known significant others. The interpersonal aspect of equity is not an issue for existence needs. The comparison process for material goods is simply among piles of goods, without necessarily attaching the added dimension of knowing who the others are who would obtain smaller or larger shares. It turns out in our society that people have learned to state such comparisons in interpersonal terms. Consequently, in developing operational definitions, some existence-need comparisons were stated as interpersonal comparisons. However, this reflects a realistic limitation of the measures, stemming from certain aspects of our culture for which the theory, not being a learning theory, does not account.

Relatedness needs involve relationships with significant other people. Family members are usually significant others, as are superiors, coworkers, subordinates, friends, and enemies. One of the basic characteristics of relatedness needs is that their satisfaction depends on a process of sharing or mutuality. People are assumed to satisfy relatedness needs by mutually sharing their thoughts and feelings. Acceptance, confirmation, understanding, and influence are elements of the relatedness process. Significant others include groups as well as individuals. Any human unit can become a significant other for a person if he has sustained interaction with this person either by virtue of his own choice or because of the setting in which he is located. Families, work groups, friendship groups, and professional groups are examples of significant groups with which a person might have a relationship and therefore relatedness needs.

The theoretical roots of the relatedness concept are two-fold. One set of theorists have focussed primarily on what occurs between persons when they relate to each other. Out of this work has come Rogers' theory of interpersonal relationships (1959) and Argyris' concepts of authentic relationships and interpersonal competence (1962). Complementary to the emphasis on what happens between the parties is the attention to what happens within each person. Freudian and neo-Freudian theorists such as Sullivan (1953), Horney (1945), and Klein (1959) have given particular attention to how significant others may be represented intrapsychically and what emotions these representations may carry.

This conception of relatedness needs does not necessitate equal formal power between (or among) people for satisfaction to occur, although for some emotions, such as anger, power equalization tends to aid authentic expression. The essential conditions involve the willingness of both (or all) persons to share their thoughts and feelings as fully as possible while trying to enable the other(s) to do the same thing (Argyris, 1962). Certainly not all interpersonal relationships are characterized by the mutual sharing and concern implied by this definition. However, I wish to suggest that this is the direction toward which relationships move when people wish to be meaningfully related to each other and when the relationship is not marred by defensiveness or lack of commitment by one or more of the parties.

Furthermore, the outcome of satisfying relatedness needs need not always be a positive affectual state for both or either person. The exchange or expression of anger and hostility is a very important part of meaningful interpersonal relationships, just as is the expression of warmth and closeness. Thus, the opposite of relatedness satisfaction is not necessarily anger, but it is a sense of distance or lack of connection.

A major difference between relatedness and existence needs arises under conditions of scarcity with respect to either satisfaction. For existence needs, a limited supply of material goods can result in one party being highly satisfied if, for example, he obtains all or nearly all of the scarce supply. However, for relatedness satisfaction a scarce supply is hypothesized to affect both parties in similar ways. That is to say, if a relationship is not working, both (or all) parties suffer. This is not to say that the parties suffer equally. The relationship may be more central for one of the parties than for the other. However, the degree of suffering or satisfaction among the parties always tends to be positively correlated for relatedness needs. For existence needs, however, the degree of suffering among parties tends to be inversely related when there is scarcity and uncorrelated when there is no scarcity.

Growth needs impel a person to make creative or productive effects on himself and the environment. Satisfaction of growth needs comes from a person engaging problems which call upon him to utilize his capacities fully and may include requiring him to develop additional capacities. A person experiences a greater sense of whole-ness and fullness as a human being by satisfying growth needs. Thus, satisfaction of growth needs depends on a person finding the opportunities to be what he is most fully and to become what he can. This concept owes much to the existential psychologists, such as Maslow (1954), Allport (1955), and Rogers (1961); the ego-oriented psycho-analysts such as Fromm (1947) and White (1963); and the laboratory psychologists concerned with a varied experi-ence, curiosity, and activation (Harlow, 1953; Fiske and Maddi, 1961; and Scott, 1966).

Specific growth needs are defined in terms of environmental set-tings with which a person contends. Barker's (1968, p. 11) work on the ecological environment offers a relatively precise definition of what is meant here by environmental settings.

The ecological environment of a person's molar behavior, the molar environment, consists of bounded, physical-temporal locales and varie-gated but stable patterns in the behavior of people en masse.

Most people's lives contain several environmental settings in the form of organizational roles and leisure-time activities. Some of the settings studied in this research include jobs, college fraternity life, academic work, and extracurricular activities.

E.R.G. theory assumes that these three broad categories of needs are active in all living persons. How strong each need is is one question the theory addresses. All people are alike in that they possess some degree of each need, but they differ in the strength of their needs. There is no postulate of strict prepotency as Maslow has offered, but there are propositions relating lower-level need satisfaction to higher-level desires.

Summary Each of the three basic needs in E.R.G. theory were defined in terms of a target toward which efforts at gratification were aimed and in terms of a process through which, and only through which, satisfaction could be obtained. For existence needs, the targets were material substances, and the process was simply getting enough. When the substances are scarce, the process quickly becomes "win–lose," and one person's gain is correlated with an-other's loss. For relatedness needs, the targets were significant others (persons or groups) and the process was mutual sharing of thoughts and feelings. For growth needs, the targets were environmental settings, and there were joint processes of a person becoming more differentiated and integrated as a human being.

Propositions Relating Satisfaction to Desire

Seven major propositions in the E.R.G. theory provide a basis from which empirically testable hypotheses relating satisfaction to desire can be logically derived. The form of this derivation is as follows. If A is an operational indicator of an E., an R., or a G. satisfaction and B is an operational indicator of an E., an R., or a G. desire, then A should show an empirically verifiable relationship to B in such a way as predicted by one of the E.R.G. propositions. If empirical results provide support for the A to B relationship, then one can have more confidence in the theory. If the empirical results do not provide support for the A to B relationship, one would have less confidence in the theory. The structure of this theory is such that the results can provide support for some propositions while not for others.

The major propositions in E.R.G. theory are as follows:

*P*1. The less existence needs are satisfied, the more they will be desired.

*P*2. The less relatedness needs are satisfied, the more existence needs will be desired.

*P*3. The more existence needs are satisfied, the more relatedness needs will be desired.

*P*4. The less relatedness needs are satisfied, the more they will be desired.

*P*5. The less growth needs are satisfied, the more relatedness needs will be desired.

*P*6. The more relatedness needs are satisfied, the more growth needs will be desired.

*P*7. The more growth needs are satisfied, the more they will be desired.

These propositions indicate that any desire can have several types of satisfaction (including some outside its particular category) affecting its strength. Any satisfaction also affects more than one type of desire (including some outside its particular category). This multiple determination property is shown in Figure 2-1 which gives a summary of the propositions in diagrammatic form.

An additional aspect of the theory, however, concerns providing explanatory concepts or mechanisms which lie behind the various propositions. These explanatory concepts are intended to help answer the "why" questions for the various propositions. As such, they add richness to the theoretical framework. They may be seen as analogous to axioms which provide a basis from which the main propositions can be derived.

Figure 2–1.   Satisfaction to Desire Propositions from E.R.G. Theory*

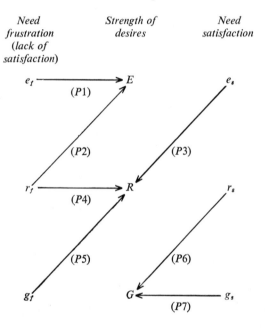

* Numbers on the Diagram refer to the proposition numbers in the text.

Within Need Categories Proposition 1, which deals with the impact of the existence need satisfaction on existence desires, has an assumption of the *interchangeability* of various satisfiers of existence needs. Pay and fringe benefits are obvious examples where an organization actually makes choices about how to compensate its employees. The investigations of Nealey (1963) and others have been based on this assumption. Where the interchangeability assumption may not be as obvious is with such things as physical working conditions or physical demands of the job. However, most job-evaluation systems contain provisions where an employee is paid more because he has dirty, hazardous, or physically taxing duties in his job (Strauss and Sayles, 1967). Moreover, Jacques (1961) has formulated a view of payment based upon the time span of discretion. According to his view, there is a correspondence between equitable payment and discretion. He reported that there is evidence to support the view that the length of discretionary time span corresponds with the financial loss which would be caused by sub-standard discretion (1961, p. 84).

Dunnette (1967) and Lawler and Porter (1963) have argued that pay can stimulate and satisfy needs other than for material goods. Lawler and Porter showed correlations between managers' pay and their esteem and autonomy satisfaction. Reasoning from expectancy theory, Dunnette suggested that pay can be used as a reward for those who seek power, status, and achievement. His view was that pay could be instrumental for satisfying these other needs.

Some of the implications of these views conflict with E.R.G. theory while others do not. According to the E.R.G. definitional system, pay is an existence need; it is a material substance which can be scarce and thereby promote a win-lose orientation among people who do not have enough. Pay *per se* cannot satisfy relatedness or growth needs but could be part of a process which results in these needs being satisfied. Giving a person a raise, for example, might be a way of communicating a feeling of esteem for him. It might also be a tactic for "keeping him quiet." Additional pay might be a way for a person to obtain greater autonomy but only if he is able to use the money to create an environmental setting conducive to his being independent and self-directive. The discussion of *P*2 will deal further with this issue.

The structure of *P*4 is similar to that of *P*1 when it states that lack of satisfaction of relatedness needs leads to higher relatedness desires. The explanatory mechanism in this proposition is *transferability* of significant others. Persons who lack a basic scheme of connectedness and sharing in their emotional lives with significant others will seek to obtain that need satisfaction. If they are unable to obtain the satisfaction with the original person where the satisfaction is missing, then they will tend to transfer the desire to others. Some of the earliest clues about the operation of this process are found in Freud's (1963, p. 106) work on transference.

Expectant libidinal impulses will inevitably be roused, in anyone whose need for love is not being satisfactorily gratified in reality, by each new person coming upon the scene, and it is more than probable that both parts of the libido, the conscious and the unconscious, will participate in this attitude.

Proposition 7 is like $P1$ and $P4$ in that it implies that satisfaction of growth needs in one environmental setting affects a person's desires in other settings. But it is also different because the sign of the relationship between satisfaction and desire is positive rather than negative. The explanatory mechanism in this proposition is the notion of *expanding* environments. Persons who experience growth in one setting tend not only to seek more opportunities in that setting but also seek more settings in which to rise and develop their talents.

Downward and Upward Movement in the Hierarchy The concepts of existence, relatedness, and growth needs were presented as separate and distinct categories. One of the ways in which the needs can be ordered, however, is on a continuum in terms of their concreteness (Harvey, Hunt, and Schroder, 1961). Existence needs are the most concrete. Their presence or absence is the easiest for the person to verify due to the fact that they can be reduced to material substances. Relatedness needs are less concrete than existence needs. Their presence or absence depends on the state of a relationship between two or more people. To verify the state of relatedness needs depends on the consensual validation of the people involved in the relationship. Finally, growth needs are the least concrete. Ultimately, their specific objectives depend on the uniqueness of each person. At the most precise level, the state of a person's growth can be fully known only to him and only when he is not deluding himself. The continuum from more to less concreteness is also a continuum from more to less verifiability and from less to more potential uncertainty for the person.

Propositions 2 and 5 follow from the concept of *frustration-regression* which played such an important part in Lewinian field theory (Barker, Dunbo, and Lewin, 1943). Regression meant a more primitive, less mature way of behaving, not necessarily behavior that had been produced earlier in life (Lewin, 1951). Frustration-regression is employed in E.R.G. theory to identify one motivational basis for explaining primitivity of some desires.

The sense in which *frustration-regression* is employed in E.R.G. theory concerns the tendency of persons to desire more concrete ends as a consequence of being unable to obtain more differentiated, less concrete ends. Thus, a person wants material substances when his relatedness needs are not satisfied because he is using them as a more concrete way of establishing his connectedness with other people. He wants relationships with significant others when his growth needs are not being met because he is using them for alternative sources of stimulation. In neither case will substitute gratification satisfy the original desire, but rationality is only part of the picture in understanding motivation.

It is in this sense that a person may use the size of his pay check as an indicator of the esteem in which he is held by his boss, colleagues, or organization. At the cultural level, Fromm (1947, p. 6) has called this kind of phenomenon the "market orientation." From her work with psychiatric patients, Horney (1937; p. 174) proposed that the neurotic quest for material possessions not only followed from anxiety about interpersonal relationships but also served as an indirect way of expressing hostility.

Propositions 3 and 6 follow from the concept of *satisfaction-progression* which played an important part in Maslow's (1954) original concept of the need hierarchy. In the case of E.R.G. theory, however, the movement up the hierarchy from relatedness satisfaction to growth desires does not presume satisfaction of existence needs. The assumption implied in the satisfaction-progression mechanism is that a person has more energy available for the more personal and less certain aspects of living if he has obtained gratification in the more concrete areas. Movement from existence satisfaction to relatedness desires is possible because a person fears others as competitors for scarce material goods less as he satisfies his existence needs. Satisfaction of relatedness needs provides a source of social support for persons seeking to develop and use their skills and talents. As his relatedness needs become satisfied, a person is freed to want to grow by a sense of greater authenticity in his relations with others.

Propositions Relating Desires to Satisfaction

Any theory that takes a position by stating that certain human characteristics (such as needs) apply to all people must also deal with the fact that people are different. Assuming that all persons have existence, relatedness, and growth needs is not the same as assuming that all people have these needs in the same degree. E.R.G. theory does not assume that all people have the same chronic strength of the various needs. However, the theory does assume that to *some* degree all people do have all three broad categories of needs.

The relationship between chronic desires and satisfaction in E.R.G. theory depends both on the particular need in question and on the nature of the material, interpersonal, and ecological conditions facing the person. The various needs and relevant conditions will be taken up according to need category. Each of the following propositions is based on the conceptual definitions of the needs, both the targets and the processes for obtaining need satisfaction.

Existence Needs Satisfaction of existence needs depends on a person's getting enough of the various material substances that he wants. When there is scarcity (as is most often the case), a person with high needs will be able to obtain a lower proportion of his desires than a person with low needs. When there is no scarcity, then everyone can get what he wants, and there would be no difference in degree of satisfaction between those with different chronic existence needs. An example can be taken from the case of oxygen, an existence need that is normally but not always in very abundant supply. When there is no shortage of oxygen, then everyone can get all he needs. People rarely express much dissatisfaction under these conditions. However, when oxygen exists in limited supply, as is true in a submarine, then those people with higher needs, such as a person with a heart condition, would suffer more as the amount available diminished than those with lower needs. To summarize:

> *P8a.* When existence materials are scarce, then the higher chronic existence desires are, the less existence satisfaction.
>
> *P8b.* When existence materials are not scarce, then there will be no differential existence satisfaction as a function of chronic existence desires.

Relatedness Needs Satisfaction of relatedness needs depends on people establishing relationships in which they can mutually share their relevant thoughts and feelings. Most people are to some degree responsive to the thoughts and feelings of others with whom they interact. Consequently, persons with varying needs almost always have the possibility of increasing the amount of mutual exchange that occurs by being more empathic and sharing more of themselves. At the same time, people differ in the degree of exchange that they want or can tolerate comfortably. These preferences set limits on the satisfaction they can obtain and also on the satisfaction others who interact with them can obtain.

In the optimally satisfying relationship, a person is able to share and be heard on all relevant matters to him. In a highly dissatisfying relationship, a person is able to share and be heard on a very small proportion of relevant issues. Persons who are very high on chronic relatedness needs may find it more difficult to achieve satisfaction under normal conditions because they may be perceived as over-whelming others with their thoughts and feelings, while persons very low on chronic relatedness needs may find it difficult to achieve satisfaction under normal conditions because they do not invest enough of themselves in the relationship for it to become very satis-fying (Storr, 1960). In a very satisfying relationship, the degree of chronic relatedness needs may have no impact on satisfaction because a person is able to establish conditions which permit him to share and be heard as much as he wants, however much that is. In a very dissatisfying relationship, a person with very high relatedness needs may be able to get more satisfaction because he is more willing to invest himself, and even the most deteriorating relationship can benefit by the efforts of one party.

In order to state these ideas in propositional form, a distinction among the three kinds of interpersonal states is employed as a moderating variable between chronic relatedness desires and related-ness satisfaction. The terms "highly satisfying," "normal," and "highly dissatisfying" are loosely defined at this point, but they do provide a point from which to begin research.

> *P9a.* In highly satisfying relationships, there is no differential related-ness satisfaction as a function of chronic relatedness desires.
> *P9b.* In normal relationships, persons very high and very low on

chronic relatedness desires tend to obtain lower satisfaction than persons with moderate desires.

P9c. In highly dissatisfying relationships, then, the higher chronic relatedness desires, the more relatedness satisfaction.

Growth Needs Satisfaction of growth needs depends on a person's being able to find ways to utilize his capabilities and to develop new talents. Ecological environments vary in the degree to which they permit or encourage the use of a person's full capabilities. Some settings contain very little opportunity for discretion and offer little stimulation or challenge. A prototypic example of this kind of setting would be an assembly-line job. Other settings offer a high degree of stimulation and choice to persons. The job of a high level executive might be a case of this type of setting. Growth satisfaction depends on a person's taking a proactive stance toward his environment, but if the setting is unresponsive, it matters little if the person wants to produce effects because he cannot. Thus, the major mediating effect of the environment concerns whether the setting offers challenge and choice.

P10a. In challenging discretionary settings, then, the higher chronic growth desires, the more growth satisfaction.

P10b. In nonchallenging, nondiscretionary settings, there will be no differential growth satisfaction as a function of chronic growth desires.

Summary and Implications By combining propositions 1 to 7 with 8 to 10, one obtains a set of answers to the questions of how need satisfaction relates to desire and how chronic desires relate to need satisfaction. According to this view, the relationship between satisfaction and desire is essentially instantaneous. As soon as a person is aware of whether his needs are being satisfied, his desires change according to the propositions outlined above. But the relationships between chronic desires and satisfaction are not instantaneous. Because of the mediating effects of external conditions, there is a time delay (of unknown degree at this time) between how quickly a person of given chronic desires obtains the possible satisfactions available to him.

The impact of combining propositions 1 and 8a is to define an existence-need deficiency cycle: Under scarcity, the less a person is satisfied the more he desires, and the more he desires the less he is satisfied. As a result a person could become fixated on material needs.

The impact of combining propositions 7 and 10a is to define a growth-need enrichment cycle: In challenging discretionary settings, the more a person is satisfied the more he desires, and the more he desires the more he is satisfied. As a result, a person who is already growth oriented is likely to become increasingly so.

Although relatedness satisfactions do not play a direct role in either of these cycles, they can play a supporting or suppressing part in both. If relatedness satisfaction decreases, then the existence desires tend to increase while growth desires tend to decrease, thereby supporting the existence deficiency cycle while suppressing the growth enrichment cycle. If relatedness satisfaction increases, growth desires tend to increase while existence desires tend to decrease, thereby supporting the growth enrichment cycle while suppressing the existence deficiency cycle. These cyclic implications are shown diagrammatically in Figure 2-2.

COMPARISON WITH OTHER THEORIES

Simple Frustration Hypothesis

There are versions of the simple frustration hypothesis which deal with both questions regarding the relationship between satisfaction and desire. When satisfaction affects desire, the formulation is that dissatisfaction increases desire, although the language is not always identical to that used here. Two formulations are those of Homans (1961) and Berkowitz (1969).

> The more often a man in the recent past received a rewarding activity from another, the less valuable any further unit of that activity becomes to him. (Homans, 1961, p. 55)

> When the deprivation is eliminated or the disturbing stimuli are bypassed, the drive state diminishes or disappears altogether. . . . (Berkowitz, 1969, p. 55)

When desire affects satisfaction, the formulation is the higher desires, the less satisfaction. Morse (1963) and Zaleznik (1966) have presented formulations.

> The greater the amount the individual gets, the greater his satisfaction and, at the same time, the more the individual still desires, the less his satisfaction. (Morse, 1953, p. 28)

Figure 2–2.   Cyclic Implications of E.R.G. Propositions*

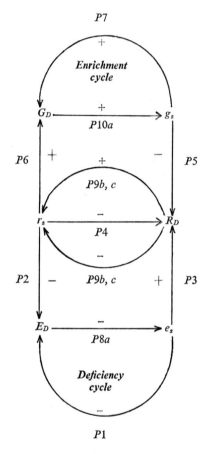

* *E,R,G,e,r,g* refer to need categories; *s,D* refer to satisfaction on desire; *P1–P10* refer to proposition numbers in the text; and the signs refer to the direction of the relationships.

Satisfaction varies directly with environmental returns and inversely with individual needs. This proposition attempts to explain why individuals vary in their degree of felt satisfaction with organizational rewards (Zaleznik, 1966, p. 208)

The simple frustration hypothesis is a more parsimonious alternative to E.R.G. theory, for it specifies no need categories and exists as a single proposition. This simplicity makes comparison with E.R.G. theory relatively easy.

To the extent that there is any empirical support for positive relationships between satisfaction and desire, the simple frustration hypothesis becomes untenable as a generalization which applies to all kinds of human needs. To the extent that there is support for relationships between one specific satisfaction and another specific desire *within* a single need category, the simple frustration hypothesis becomes incomplete. To the extent that there are relationships between satisfactions and desires across need categories, the simple frustration hypothesis becomes inadequate. E.R.G. theory contains propositions of all of these kinds (*P3*, *P6*, *P7*, *P9c*, *P10a*). Every time there is empirical support for one of them, it tends to favor this theory over the simple frustration hypothesis.

At the same time, there has been considerable empirical support for the simple frustration hypothesis as Lawson and Marx (1958) have shown. So to be a fully viable alternative to the simple frustration hypothesis, the E.R.G. theory should not only account more fully for data which the simple frustration hypothesis cannot, it should also account for the data which does support the simple frustration hypothesis. Aspects of propositions 1 and 4 do subsume the simple frustration hypothesis.

Other Ways to Conceptualize Human Needs

The business of categorizing or developing lists of human needs and motives is not a new activity. Henry Murray's (1938) list is well known. Langer (1937) and Schein (1965) have also suggested three category sets which bear considerable similarity to the one proposed in E.R.G. theory. Maslow's (1954) theory rests on a series of assumptions about how human needs might best be conceptualized. Except for Maslow's categories these other conceptualizations serve a different function than the E.R.G. system. They serve not as part of an articulated theory but as a taxonomy to be used for other purposes than understanding and explaining the relationships between satisfaction and desire.

But one may wish to use the E.R.G. categories for taxonomic purposes (such as in organizational diagnosis) as well. Here the notion is that existence, relatedness, and growth needs are basic elements which may combine to form complex goals. A person may want a promotion, for example, because it will provide him with greater material rewards, more opportunities to use his abilities, and greater possibilities for relationships with certain others than his current position. Another man may seek power in the form of greater control over material things, or greater control in interpersonal relationships, or both.

n Power, *n* Affiliation, and especially *n* Achievement have been the subject of much research as the result of the efforts of McClelland (1953), Atkinson (1958), and their colleagues. Each of these needs bears some similarity to the E.R.G. system of categories in definable ways. As defined originally by Murray (1938), *n* Power (or Dominance) and *n* Affiliation both capture aspects of the relatedness process. *n* Power refers to the exercise of influence and *n* Affiliation to the exchange of warm feelings. Each of these two represents only part of the relatedness process and obtained by itself would mean incomplete relatedness satisfaction. In a similar manner, *n* Achievement captures a part but not all of the growth process. Exercising one's abilities in the pursuit of challenging goals and achieving those goals is certainly part of increasing one's sense of capacity as a person. But there are more ways of obtaining a greater sense of wholeness and integration than through success alone. Zaleznik (1967), for example, has documented ways that failure can also be an opportunity for growth, if one is able to face it and learn from it.

Maslow's Theory

There are four general ways in which E.R.G. theory differs from Maslow's (1954) theory. These major differences in turn lead to the theories' making different predictions at a number of points. In some cases, E.R.G. theory makes predictions where Maslow's theory makes none. The differences concern (1) how the categories of needs are formed, (2) the presence or absence of a strict prepotency assumption, (3) how frustration of higher-order needs affects lower-order desires, and (4) how chronic desires relate to satisfaction.

Differences in Need Categories Maslow's theory deals with five sets of needs: Physiological, safety, love, esteem, and self-actualization. But there tends to be some ambiguity among these categories. It appears that safety needs overlap with both physiological needs and love needs.   In his discussion of the safety concept, Maslow mentions issues such as physical illness, pain, and assault as one set of issues and parental outbursts of rage, name calling, and speaking harshly as another. E.R.G. theory proposes that physical threats might be usefully put together with Maslow's physiological category and, thereby, fit the existence need category.   Safety issues involving

Figure 2-3.   Comparison of Maslow and E.R.G. Concepts

Maslow *categories*	*E.R.G.* *categories*
Physiological	Existence
Safety-material	
Safety-interpersonal	Relatedness
Love (belongingness)	
Esteem—interpersonal	
Esteem—self-confirmed	Growth
Self-actualization	

interaction with other people would be considered part of love needs and, thereby, included with relatedness needs.

A similar point applies to Maslow's esteem needs.   In this case the overlap is with love and self-actualization needs.   Maslow indicates that his concept of esteem includes the regard a person receives from others.   In this sense, it is very similar to love needs.   However, he goes on to refer to that aspect of esteem which depends on the internal cues from real capacity, achievement, and independence with which a person provides himself. This element of esteem seems to be more like self-actualization. Here E.R.G. theory proposes that those aspects of esteem which depend upon reactions from others he included with relatedness needs while those which represent autonomous, self-fulfilling activity fit with growth needs.

Maslow's physiological needs readily fit with E.R.G.'s existence needs, his love (or belongingness) needs with E.R.G.'s relatedness needs, and his self-actualization needs with E.R.G.'s growth needs. Therefore, E.R.G. theory proposes that Mastow's safety and esteem needs be decomposed to fit the E.R.G. categories, while accepting Maslow's other three needs essentially as they are. Figure 2-3 shows the comparison diagrammatically.

In the case of esteem relatedness needs, the change in categorization speaks to a problem that Maslow himself noted (1943, p. 386):

There are some people in whom, for instance, self-esteem seems to be more important than love. This most common reversal in the hierarchy is usually due to the development of the notion that the person who is most likely to be loved is a strong or powerful person. . . .

By recognizing that part of self-esteem which depends on regard from others as part of relatedness needs, the issue of whether love desires precede or follow desires for the esteem of others vanishes.

Another type of general difference between E.R.G. concepts and Maslow's concepts is that the E.R.G. definitions contain a formula for identifying specific needs in each category, while generally speaking Maslow's definitions do not. One exception is Maslow's discussion of love and interpersonal safety needs where he does mention specific individuals and groups. Especially in the discussion of self-actualization needs, however, the notion of specifying different settings for obtaining satisfaction is not present. Consequently, the self-actualization concept tends to have unnecessary connotations of teleology or self-indulgence. By identifying the role of ecological environments, the growth concept recognizes the role of factors external to a person not only in supporting his growth but also in stimulating it. The skills and talents a person may wish to use and develop depend not only on his innate characteristics but also on the challenges and opportunities provided by the specific settings in which he finds himself.

E.R.G. theory's specification of separate needs in each category also has effects on operationalizing the concepts, as we shall see in Chapter 5.

The Presence or Absence of a Strict Prepotency Assumption E.R.G. theory retains the notion of a need hierarchy without requiring it to be strictly ordered. Maslow says that for a chronically hungry man "life tends to be defined in terms of eating. Anything else will be defined as unimportant" (1943, p. 374). E.R.G. theory would say that a chronically hungry man can recognize whether he feels connected to primary groups and to society and whether he is able to engage in activities which enable him to use his skills and talents. E.R.G. propositions 3 and 6 have the same orientation as Maslow's hierarchy, but they do not require lower level gratification as an additional condition as Maslow's theory does.

The absence of a strictly ordered hierarchy in E.R.G. theory also meets a criticism that Maslow himself (1943, p. 386) raised about his theory.

There are other, apparently innately creative people in whom the drive to creativeness seems to be more important than any other counter-determinant. Their creativeness might appear not as self-actualization released by basic satisfaction, but in spite of lack of basic satisfaction.

How Frustration of Higher-Order Needs Affects Lower-Order Desires Maslow made the point that "needs cease to play an active determining or organizing role as soon as they are gratified" (1943, p. 393). E.R.G. theory has a different point of view. One way in which a satisfied need can remain a motivator is if it is activated through serving as a substitute for some other need which itself is not being fully satisfied. E.R.G. theory contains two propositions of this kind. They involve the need hierarchy principle working in reverse; if a higher-order need is frustrated, the next lower order need is activated. E.R.G. propositions 2 and 5 state:

P2. The less relatedness needs are satisfied, the more existence needs will be desired.
P5. The less growth needs are satisfied, the more relatedness needs will be desired.

Neither these propositions nor others similar to them are found in Maslow's work.

How Chronic Desires Relate to Satisfaction   E.R.G. theory attempts to deal not only with how satisfaction affects desire but also with how chronic desires affect satisfaction by using the same set of concepts.   Maslow's theory does not deal with the second question at all.   Consequently, the degree of empirical support which is found for propositions 8 to 10 represents another way of differentiating between the theories.

Summary and Implications   Maslow's basic hypothesis is that a certain degree of satisfaction of lower-level needs is a prerequisite for the appearance of higher-order needs.   Operating from this general hypothesis, the threefold categorization implies some different predictions from the fivefold conceptualization.   Stating these different predictions utilizes the distinctions within Maslow's need categories which are shown in Figure 2-3.

According to Maslow's original system, the more physiological satisfaction, the *more* safety desires.   According to the E.R.G. analysis, additional propositions would be necessary to deal with the relationship between physiological satisfaction and safety desires. They would be:

a. The more physiological satisfaction, the *less* material-safety desires.

b. The more material-safety satisfactions, the *more* interpersonal-safety desires.

c. The more physiological satisfaction, the *more* interpersonal-safety desires.

According to Maslow's system, the more belongingness satisfaction, the *more* esteem desires (provided there was adequate satisfaction of physiological and safety needs).   Again the E.R.G. analysis would require additional propositions to cover the same phenomena.   They would be:

a. The more belongingness satisfaction, the *less* interpersonal-esteem desires (given adequate lower-level need satisfaction).

b. The more interpersonal-esteem satisfaction, the *more* self-confirmed esteem desires (given adequate lower-level need satisfaction).

c. The more belongingness satisfaction, the more self-confirmed esteem desires (given adequate lower-level need satisfaction).

In both of these cases, the E.R.G. conceptualization raises the possibility that failure to find support for some of Maslow's propositions concerning middle-level needs could stem from inadequate conceptualization. An analysis which combined the effects of the *a* and *b* propositions above would tend to result in a null finding because effects operating in opposite directions would cancel each other without an investigator's knowing it.

In this chapter E.R.G. theory was described in its own terms. The leading alternative views—the simple frustration hypothesis and Maslow's theory—were also presented. Differences between the alternative approaches were identified and, where possible, differential predictions were specified.

Chapter 3

BACKGROUND

Few ideas or theories emerge from a vacuum. Most concepts have an intellectual history of some kind. In the area of motivation, it is not at all surprising to find the roots of many ideas in the writings of Greek philosophers. Certain psychoanalytic concepts can be recognized in Shakespearean plays. Investigators in behavioral science tend to share norms about what events may be accepted as evidence. It is not unusual, for example, for reviewers of the literature to specify crucial criteria (such as, the study must be a laboratory experiment) for it to be included in a report on the literature in a certain area. Such criteria are most appropriate when one's goal is assessing the validity of some empirical generalization.

This chapter presents the major sources of data which lend support to the central theoretical ideas in this book. Several sources of evidence, emerging from quite divergent traditions of study, may lend support to the plausibility of a model if convergence among the results is found. The type of material to be considered ranges from studies which are highly rigorous and controlled to much "looser" interventions in ongoing organizations. When one can see evidence of agreement from sources so different, then the plausibility of a conceptual framework which speaks to the commonalities among the various findings increases. First, we shall deal with the material which has pointed to the formulation of E.R.G. theory and then review the empirical literature pertaining to tests of Maslow's theory.

E.R.G. THEORY

Need Categories

There is evidence from several sources that human needs may be fruitfully conceptualized in terms of three conceptually independent categories: material existence needs, interpersonal relatedness needs, and personal growth needs.

Three sources of evidence provide the major support for this assertion: (1) Several lines of systematic research on the functioning of motives in animals and men; (2) the major thrust of several types of organizational change programs; and (3) the results of numerous factor analytic studies of employee attitudes.

To establish that a particular category of needs is independent of other categories is to show that an organism requires that particular type of gratification for its own sake. This is to say that the organism does not learn to value a particular end state only because it has been paired with other "more basic" needs. He does not seek a particular goal only because it is instrumental for reaching some other higher priority end. He seeks it for its own sake. Without obtaining the particular goal, the organism may be impeded or permanently retarded in its normal development. Without the need being satisfied, the organism may show behavior uncharacteristic of effectively functioning members of its species, or it may not show other behavior which is characteristic of effectively functioning members of its species.

Existence Needs So much of experimental psychology is based on the assumption of the primacy of certain material needs— especially hunger and thirst—that it may strike some investigators as self-evident that these needs are independent and essential for people to survive and grow. We all know that extreme deprivation of food, water, heat, etc. can lead to death. What happens when the derpivation is not that extreme?

Holmberg (1960) studied the Siriono Indians of Eastern Bolivia, a society in which the drive for food is so constantly frustrated that it became the dominant motivating factor, according to the investigator. The natives' behavior seemed unmistakable in its meaning. Food was hastily prepared. There were no complex recipes, standardized or ritualized routines for eating, or decided food preferences— except for more. People stole off into the forest to eat, wolfed their food, over-ate when food was available, and were quite reluctant to share food. They ate when not hungry, when they were sick, and quarreled excessively about food. Their fantasies and dreams were about food, and they insulted one another in terms of food.

The investigator saw the outstanding personality traits of the Siriono as aggressiveness, individualism, and uncooperativeness. They tended to be highly independent and showed a formidable apathy toward their fellow men. However, while meaningful relationships were rare, cooperation among people was not totally absent. Hunters cooperated in the jungle. When on the move, men helped women carry the family burdens. Family members collaborated in building dwellings and planted gardens in common. A man wishing to approach a potential wife might send food to her by means of an intermediary.

An unusual experiment was carried out by Franklin, Schiele, Brozek, and Keys (1948) in which over the period of a year they controlled quite carefully the food consumption of thirty-six volunteer male subjects. The experiment lasted for one year. During the first three months control data was obtained on a "good" diet of about 3,500 calories per man per day. The next six months were given to semi-starvation conditions in which the average daily intake was reduced to about 1,600 calories per man. The semi-starvation period was followed by a three month rehabilitation period. The reported effects of semi-starvation were marked. Fatigue, weakness, and hunger were outstanding complaints. Frequently, the men complained of hunger immediately after having eaten a bulky meal. There was a desire for warmth in the food which was eaten. In general, tolerance for heat was increased, or put another way, heat was desired more than usual. Men tended to take a highly possessive attitude toward their food, and they became easily irritated when those serving the food moved slowly or did not take their "business" seriously enough. Other intakes were substituted for food; coffee, tea, chewing gum, and cigarettes were desired more than usual. People became preoccupied with food. There were more dreams about food, and in general, people simply noticed food issues more. At the same time as they collected recipes and cooking utensils, people became generally more possessive, thinking, for instance, about saving money for a "rainy day".

A general pattern might be noticed in these data. The specific object of deprivation, food, became decidedly more important. But so did other material and physiological gratifications: Food substitutes like tea, coffee, and so on; warmth in many senses, including heat in the little food which they obtained; and money. The fact that the food deprivation seemed to lead to increased desires for other nonhunger-reducing materials gives some support to the idea of a general existence need category.

The way in which one kind of material deprivation can influence desires for others is also shown in Moskos' (1969) study of American soldiers in Vietnam. In combat the soldier lives under extreme physical conditions. He is an absolutely deprived person, struggling primarily to maximize his chances for survival. When asked what makes America different from other countries, about two-thirds of the respondents answered in materialistic terms: high paying jobs, automobiles, consumer goods, and leisure activities.

Jezernik (1968) reported on the relative importance of a number of factors which influenced workers in Slovenia, Yugoslavia. In 1962, he found that the rank of wages in six different factories was highly correlated with the ratio of realized incomes to aspired incomes. The higher the ratio, the lower the rank given to the importance of wages. Satisfaction with wages was also inversely correlated with importance of wages for individuals.

Lawler and Porter (1963) report from a large-scale study of executives that the more pay a manager received the less important pay was for him. They also report that satisfaction with pay increased with actual amount of pay. Although the writers do not directly report it, one could infer from their data that the importance of pay decreased the more satisfied a manager was with his pay.

Lawson and Marx (1958) completed an extensive review of the literature on theory and experiment on frustration. The studies dealt with many kinds of frustration—delayed reward, extinction, interruption of response sequence, and so on—and covered studies based on both animal and human subjects. One of their general conclusions from the review is: "Frustration often increases motivation." These authors did not make distinctions between types of needs, but it probably would be fair to suggest that their conclusion applies to all the need categories. It might also be noted that more experimental studies have been done with existence needs than with others.

Studies of the factor structure of employee attitudes repeatedly show the presence of factors which may be characterized as specific material needs. Ten studies have found a factor labeled pay (Dabas, 1958; Roach, 1958; Wherry, 1958; Kahn, 1960; Baehr, 1954; Wherry, 1954; Ash, 1954; Harrison, 1960; Harrison, 1961; and Hinrichs, 1968). Eight studies have shown a factor called working conditions (Dabas, 1958; Wherry, 1958; Will and King, 1965; Twery, Schmid, and Wrigley, 1958; Baehr, 1954; Wherry, 1954; Harrison, 1960; Harrison, 1961). Four studies resulted in a factor called fringe benefits (Dabas, 1958; Ash, 1954; Harrison, 1960; Harrison, 1961).

At the outset of its development, the labor movement sought mainly the opportunity to secure a better material state for its members. In the words of Samuel Gompers (1919, p. 20):

The ground-work principle of America's labor movement has been to recognize that first things come first. The primary essential in our mission has been the protection of the wage-worker, now; to increase his wages; to cut hours off the long workday, which was killing him; to improve the safety and the sanitary conditions of the work-shop; to free him from the tyrannies, petty or otherwise, which served to make his existence a slavery.

After gains had been made in legitimizing labor's voice in the state of its own material welfare, there arose, among a relatively small set of organizations, a program which was designed to bring together the two camps of labor and management into a more mature relationship. This program was initiated largely by Joseph Scanlon, first a labor leader and later a lecturer in Industrial Relations at M.I.T. When the Scanlon plan worked, it resulted in less divisiveness between labor and management. Labor received the savings in labor costs which it could effect in the form of additional take-home pay (Lesieur, 1958).

The results of these many studies lend support to formulation of material existence needs as a basic element in human motivation. Included in this conceptualization is the idea that specific needs may be defined in terms of particular material objects and that scarcity in one particular area may affect desires not only for that object but for others as well. E.R.G. theory does not include physiological variables but a psychological state of desire for a particular material object may be affected by scarcity of some other material object.

Relatedness Needs Material needs are probably the only ones that could be postulated independently without having to dispose of alternative arguments as to their source. Principally, these arguments would suggest that additional needs arise because organisms transform more basic needs or learn new needs from their being associated with the satisfaction of material wants. Especially in the case of interpersonal or social needs, certain theoretical arguments tended not to view them as innately part of an organism (Murray, 1964).

Psychoanalytic theory tended to view motives other than those for sex and aggression (broadly defined) as sublimations of the more basic desires, in response to the restrictions of society. S-R (stimulus-response) learning theorists have argued that motives other than the basic material ones are acquired as a result of being paired with the more basic motives. On the subject of social needs, however, the alternative explanations have been dealt an especially hard blow by the research of Harlow (1959, 1962).

The argument for learned or acquired social motives states that social attachments develop because the social stimulus is present when material needs are being satisfied. Using monkeys as subjects, Harlow constructed two types of surrogate mothers: A wire mother and a cloth mother. Some monkeys were fed by the wire mother, others by the cloth mother. According to arguments about acquired social motives, the monkeys fed by the wire mother should have preferred her to the cloth mother. They did not. Regardless of whether a monkey was fed from the wire mother or the cloth mother, he tended to prefer the cloth mother. When fearful stimuli were presented to the monkeys, the cloth mother tended to be sought after for security and comfort, regardless of which surrogate mother had provided food earlier.

During the studies, Harlow raised some monkeys in complete isolation from either mothers or mates. These animals showed striking evidence of abnormality. At the approach of human strangers, they would direct attacks against themselves, frequently by biting. Though clearly not without a sexual drive, they proved quite incompetent in carrying out the act. They tended to remain highly withdrawn from their mates whenever they were put together.

To further understand the effects of social isolation, Harlow raised some monkeys with their mothers only and others with isolation, except for a daily period of 20 minutes in which they were permitted to play with their mates in a room richly endowed with toys. The monkeys raised only with their mothers tended to show signs of abnormality similar to the groups raised in isolation—especially the males. Those raised in isolation, except for the 20-minute play periods, showed retarded development, but eventually showed behavior which was quite similar to their normally raised mates in terms of playmate and sexual behaviors.

Harlow's studies tend to support a number of points about social needs. The results from monkeys raised in complete isolation tend to say that social gratifications are necessary for normal development. The results from the cloth mother–wire mother experiment suggest quite strongly that social attachments are not learned only in response to gratification of hunger needs. The results from the mother-only and mate-only partial isolation studies tend to say that the more important type of relationship for normal development tends to be one of mutuality.

The results from Harlow's studies show a high likelihood of being capable of generalization to other species. Scott (1967) has reported similar findings for dogs. Bowlby (1965) has become well known for his views that a child's mental health depends very much on a continuous warm and mutually intimate relationship with his mother or mother substitute. He based this view on an extensive review of literature covering many types of "maternal deprivation." These studies not only showed that absence of this type of mothering relationship seemed to retard the emotional, physical, and intellectual development of children but also that restoration of adequate mothering seemed to diminish ill effects. More recently the concept of maternal deprivation has been sharpened, and the kinds of outcome variables have been differentiated.

Ainsworth (1965) noted that maternal deprivation can be separated into insufficient interaction, distorted interaction, and discontinuity of relations. Each of these terms represents a part of the relatedness concept. Insufficient interaction pertains to the frequency of satisfaction. Distorted interaction deals with whether the relationship is mutually satisfying, and discontinuity of relations concerns whether the maternal relationship is with the same or different significant others.

Bettelheim's (1969) study of the Israeli kibbutzim addressed the question of varying significant others. It was especially concerned with whether a group can be realistically substituted for an individual mother in early childhood. At the outset of his study, he noted that he was prompted to undertake the investigation because he felt that Bowlby's (1965) views had been overstated. Perhaps institutions had failed as mother substitutes because of the kind of relationships they established with children, not because they were intrinsically ill-suited to satisfying the relationship needs of infants. As a clinician, Bettelheim had seen many children who had mothers and still lived with highly dissatisfactory relationships. His initial hypothesis was that group nurturance had not worked because it had been executed ineffectively. In the kibbutz, he found children who were quite healthy along several dimensions. Drugs, crime, sexual deviation, and neurosis were almost nonexistent. Children raised in a kibbutz had very different relationships with their parents than is common in our culture. From their earliest days, they saw their parents for brief periods each day while their primary care was charged to professionals called *metapelets*, and they spent most of their time with children of their own age. Children raised in this manner in the kibbutzim showed less pathology according to Bettelheim's observations but they also showed less individualism and tended to be somewhat flat emotionally. The community was a key significant other for them. Some quantitative data showed that more of these children were in the middle ranges on educational achievement tests and fewer were on either extreme than children raised by more traditional methods. These findings seem to suggest that significant others may be satisfactorily substituted. Groups, to a degree, may replace individuals as mothers. At the same time, they do not suggest that all of the consequences will be identical.

Some writers (e.g., Rabkin and Rabkin, 1969) have tended to treat the kibbutz research as if it represented a point of view contradictory to Bowlby. If one chooses to view Bowlby as making a case that the only way for a child to mature is through a warm mutual relationship with a single mothering person, then the kibbutz findings are contradictory. But if one chooses to view Bowlby's work as making a case that some kinds of emotional qualities are necessary in a child's relationship with significant others for him to mature, then the kibbutz results provide a basis for enriching and elaborating these views without contradicting the main points.

Zigler, Balla, and Butterfield (1968) found that familial mental retardates with histories of social deprivation showed greater motivation for social reinforcement than those without histories of social deprivation. Over a three-year period of being institutionalized, those children with more social deprivation showed a greater decrease in motivation than those with less deprivation. These results replicated an earlier study by Zigler and Williams (1963) which had been carried out in a different institution.

While Zigler's research utilized historical conditions for the independent variable of social deprivation, another series of investigators have created conditions of social isolation in the laboratory to test its effect on social motivation. As in Zigler's studies, these investigators used performance on an experimental learning task as a measure of social motivation. Gewirtz and Baer (1958a; 1958b) found that learning occurred more rapidly after children had been isolated in comparison to a control group and less rapidly after they had been satiated in comparison to a control group. Walters and Parke (1964) did additional elaborations on the Gewirtz–Baer technique in order to test the hypothesis that emotional arousal was a better explanatory variable than social isolation. They interpreted their results as supporting the alternative hypothesis. Hill and Stevenson (1964) also considered the alternative of stimulus deprivation in contrast to social deprivation and found some support for their views.

Controversy remains around the "social isolation" results, but the basis of the disagreement turns in part on the conceptual label one uses for a particular experimental condition. Walters and Parke (1964) manipulated a variable they called threat by whether their experimenter was brusque or friendly to children. One could make a case that this behavior was a more effective manipulation of relatedness satisfaction than simply leaving the children alone.

Another aspect of the laboratory studies is the use of a learning task to measure motivation rather than asking a person to report his desires. On the one hand, this procedure produces "harder" data in the form of behavior. On the other hand, one must be more inferential in reasoning backward from the observed behavior to the presence of particular desires. Moreover, one would expect that the desire would not be acted upon under all circumstances, as the results of Walters and Henning (1962) seem to show. In the usual laboratory experiment (especially with children), one finds very little evidence that mutuality of exchange ever occurs (Argyris, 1968). As a result, this writer would question whether any of the experiments have produced manipulations which produce relatedness satisfaction. So far at least, the social psychology laboratory has been a setting where different degrees of dissatisfactory relationships have been produced but hardly a situation where gratification with mutuality in human relationships needs have been created as an experimental treatment.

That natural human relationships tend to move toward mutuality has been shown in Newcomb's (1963) research. For two successive years, two sets of students lived together and were subjects of study. Both sets of people showed a general tendency toward reciprocation in their dyadic attraction with each other. Moreover, reciprocation tended to increase during the year for both groups studied. The only cases where reciprocation was notably absent were those dyads which included very popular or very unpopular people.

A study by Newman (1948) is relevant to the place of interpersonal needs in an organizational setting. The study presented a questionnaire to subjects from a sample of 1,115 nonsupervisory and 100 supervisory employees in the air transport industry. They were asked to rank nine job factors in the order of importance to them. From the total sample the investigator selected the 176 who ranked "Having an understanding and friendly supervisor" first. He then compared the results of this subsample with the remainder of the subjects in terms of their responses to a number of items dealing with interpersonal relations: (a) How well the supervisor understood the difficulties in their jobs, (b) how much favoritism there was in the shop or section, (c) how free people were to ask questions of their supervisor on difficult matters, (d) how fair treatment was, (e) what the chances were of getting a hearing and square deal on a cause for dissatisfaction, and (f) how much a part of the department the person was made to feel. Every one of these items turned out to be significantly less satisfactory for the people who rated the supervisory importance item first, than for the remainder of the sample. One might think of the first five items as dealing with satisfaction of respect by superiors and the last one as concerning respect by co-workers. The people who tended to have relationship problems with their superior or peers tended to place more importance on having a good relationship with their supervisor.

Factor analytic studies of employee attitudes repeatedly show the presence of factors which may characterize relationships with specific significant others. Thirteen studies show the presence of a factor termed immediate supervision (Dabas, 1958; Roach, 1958; Wherry, 1958; Gordon, 1955; Will and King, 1965; F. Twery, Schmid, and Wrigley, 1958; H. Kahn, 1960; Baehr, 1954; Ash, 1954; Wherry, 1954; Harrison, 1960; Harrison, 1961; Hinrichs, 1968). Seven studies show the presence of a factor called higher management (Dabas, 1958; Roach, 1958; Wherry, 1958; F. Twery, Schmid, and Wrigley, 1958; Ash, 1954; Wherry, 1954; Harrison, 1961). Six studies show a factor termed coworkers (Dabas, 1958; Roach, 1958; F. Twery, Schmid, and Wrigley, 1958; Baehr, 1954; Ash, 1954; Hinrichs, 1968). The significant others in these studies may not always be a single person, but terms like "higher management" or "coworkers" refer to an identifiable group.

Laboratory education is a recent innovation designed to help participants learn about interpersonal relationships and group dynamics (Bradford, Benne, and Gibb, 1964). Most applications of sensitivity training rely on the T-group as a primary vehicle for learning. This group typically consists of 10 to 12 participants meeting with a staff member with the purpose of studying the evolving dynamics of their own group with the goals of increasing their self-awareness, emotional insight, and interpersonal competence. One of the places where sensitivity training has had a wide application is in efforts to improve the kind of emotional-interpersonal climate in organizational settings (Argyris, 1962). Results of research on laboratory training indicate that participants, upon returning to their organizations, are seen as more aware of their behavior, more sensitive to others, more acceptant of others, and more tolerant of new information (Bunker, 1965). They also tend to use more interpersonal categories in perceiving others (Harrison, 1962). This organizational intervention was designed to aid people in organizational settings to establish more satisfactory relationships with each other, and for this end has been shown to have some success.

The case for independent and autonomous relatedness needs arising from the innate characteristics of the human animal is strong. Studies of both man and animals indicate that prolonged absence of interpersonal satisfactions severely diminish a human being's capacity to function. Field and laboratory studies have shown that deprivation of these satisfactions is associated with increased desires. The findings have also indicated that organisms can or will seek to transfer among significant others when unsatisfied needs are present and the opportunities are provided.

Growth Needs For some reason, investigators turned to trying to understand phenomena such as curiosity, manipulation, and exploration with greater ease than they did to social motivation. Nevertheless, the task that had to be undertaken was to show that desires of this sort were independent of the more basic material needs. How did the evidence accumulate for this third set of motivations? White (1959) has provided a thorough discussion of the reasons why motives of this kind cannot be explained as products of secondary reinforcement or of anxiety reduction.

The pattern of mammalian infancy seems to work against exploration developing as a product of secondary reinforcement. Babies gratify their desires for food by following a regular, routine pattern to the mother's breast. Exploration and curiosity are rather at odds with efforts to secure food. Could exploratory motives be explained as nothing more than efforts at fear reduction? An experiment by Montgomery and Monkman (1955) showed that fear in rats decreased their exploration in a novel situation. It is not too unreasonable to see fear and exploration as logically as well as behaviorally contradictory.

Challenge represents one end of a continuum. Monotony is the other. Heron, Doane, and Scott (1956, as cited by Cofer and Appley, 1964) used themselves as subjects and remained in isolation for six days. From this and similar studies it was found that subjects experience boredom, restlessness, irritability, emotional lability, and a general desire to end the experience. It was not uncommon for them to report hallucinatory activity.

Studies of reactions to highly repetitive or vigilance tasks showed similar results (Fiske, 1961). Typically subjects showed decrements in performance soon after the monotonous task began. Among the subjective reactions were boredom, unpleasantness, fatigue, irritability, restlessness, and daydreaming. These adverse conditions appear to lead people to want more challenging, stimulating, and interesting settings. Indeed, it also appears that organisms seek to increase the novelty and complexity that they experience. Montgomery (1954, as cited by White, 1959) found that rats would select the arm of a complex maze, which would increase their opportunities to explore. A shorter arm of the maze, which would more easily satisfy the need, was not selected as often as the more complex one.

Earlier work bearing on growth needs was found in Barker, Lewin, and Dembo's (1943) research on frustration and regression and in Wright's (1943) follow-up study using the same paradigm. The experimental procedure consisted of an initial meeting where the children could play with all the toys present and a second meeting in which they began by being allowed to play with all the toys but then were prevented from playing with the richest toys by a wire screen that enabled them to see but not use the more elaborate items. Constructiveness of play was rated for the children's behavior. High constructiveness scores were given for play that had complex organization, wide usage of materials, and planning. A decrease in the constructiveness of the children's play from free play to frustration was observed. The greater the frustration, the less complexity of organization, usage of materials, and planning the children showed. The effect was highly significant in both studies, showing, apparently, that the less the children were allowed to make use of their abilities, the less they played constructively.

Kornhauser's (1965) study of the mental health of industrial workers also contained relevant data. From lengthy interviews at the workers' homes, he coded a variable termed "active life orientation," which might also be called desire for growth. Data from his study, covering both a young and a middle-aged sample, showed that the proportion of the sample who received high scores on the variable increased as the skill level of their jobs increased for both young and middle-aged workers.

Similar findings emerged from Porter's (1964) national survey of managerial job attitudes. He found that as the level in the organization increased from lower management to president, dissatisfaction with autonomy and self-actualization needs showed a perfectly corresponding decrease. But the importance of both of these needs increased exactly as dissatisfaction decreased and organizational level increased. Similar findings did not hold for the other needs such as social, esteem, and security, which Porter investigated.

Like findings are given by Vroom (1964) who reports on work by Slater (1959). In this study, workers were asked how likely it was that they would think about job-related problems after work. Answers to this question were found to be related to both management ratings of aptitude required for the work and to the workers' reports of the amount of self-determination on the job. Workers whose jobs had high aptitude requirements and who had considerable opportunity for self-determination were more likely to think about work-related problems after work than were employees whose jobs had low aptitude requirements and little perceived chance for self-determination.

From the factor analytic studies of employee attitudes, there are nine studies which show a factor labeled intrinsic job satisfaction (Dabas, 1958; Roach, 1958; Wherry, 1958; Will and King, 1965; F. Twery, Schmid, and Wrigley, 1958; Kahn, 1960; Baehr, 1954; Harrison, 1960; and Hinrichs, 1968).

In industrial settings, some attention has been given to the fact that extreme division of labor in the form of various types of assembly-line technology has resulted in the creation of many lower-level jobs which have consequences for employees very similar to the results of the stimulus-deprivation research noted above. In an effort to combat some of the adverse consequences, programs of job enlargement have been undertaken by some firms in the United States and Great Britain. Typically, the results of these experiments show that overall job satisfaction as well as intrinsic job satisfaction were higher in the enlarged jobs when they are compared to analogous, more delimited jobs. Frequently productivity, as well, was higher in the enlarged jobs (Friedmann, 1961).

Convergence of evidence from a number of sources using a variety of methodologies supports the utilization of growth needs as a viable concept. Specific growth settings have also been implicitly defined, depending on the persons studied and the setting where the study took place. Play materials for children, mazes for rats, and jobs for employees formed ecological environments which satisfied growth needs to varying degrees. When growth needs were satisfied, increased desires tended to follow.

For each category of human needs proposed by E.R.G. theory, there exists empirical evidence which makes a strong case that the need is an innate quality of the human animal. Persistent deprivation in any of the areas tends to produce an organism whose functioning is markedly impaired. The organizational changes growing out of the labor movement, laboratory education, and job-enrichment programs testify to the scope and persistence of these needs.

Desires as a Function of Satisfaction

Existence Satisfaction and Relatedness Desires The experiment on semi-starvation which was outlined above provides data on this relationship. When the effects of food deprivation began to show their effect, the writers report that "social initiative decreased." Earlier urges to have a say in the conduct of nonscientific aspects of the study decreased among the subjects. People spent more and more time alone. Humor and high morale disappeared. Sexual interests declined. The number of dates had by the subjects was markedly reduced. Some of the men were surprised to find this was true even in those cases where their female contacts had appeared to be based on intellectual, social, and group interests. Such situations no doubt stemmed from a decline in sociability as well as loss of sexual impulses.

When the rehabilitation period took effect, quite different behavior patterns were observed. Morale initially went up and then declined. But this was really the first sign of the subjects regaining social initiative. They began, once again, to want more say in the conduct of the experiment. Humor, enthusiasm, and sociability progressively reappeared; irritability and nervousness diminished.

This evidence is consistent with the proposition that frustration of existence needs decreases relatedness desires.

Relatedness Satisfaction and Growth Desires Earlier, Harlow's studies (1959; 1962) with raising monkeys by surrogate mothers were discussed. At one point in these investigations, the experimenter attempted to see the consequences of placing baby monkeys who had been raised by the surrogate mothers in a large cage filled with toys which were normally quite attractive to baby monkeys. When placed in such a setting the surrogate-raised monkeys, if alone, hovered in a corner and showed little desire to play or explore their surroundings. However, when a cloth mother was placed in the playroom with them, they went to the mother, cuddling and climbing about. After some time doing this, they then ventured out to explore the setting and play with the toys.

Carl Rogers (1959, 1961) has frequently discussed what he feels are the key conditions for change to take place in psychotherapy. These conditions include sensitive empathy, unconditional positive regard, and congruence from the therapist with respect to his reactions and a relationship where these qualities are perceived to some degree by the client. He has reported some evidence indicating that if these conditions are met, positive therapeutic change does result. It would seem that for change to occur, the patient would have to want to grow or to self-actualize. Perhaps the reason that the relationship with the therapist makes a difference in therapeutic outcomes is because the proper conditions of the relationship tend to release desires for growth in the patient.

Using the paradigm of Barker, Dembo, and Lewin's (1943) study of frustration and regression, Wright (1943) investigated the effects of friendships among children on constructiveness in play. Seventy-eight children, aged 3 to 6 years, served as subjects for the study. There were 18 pairs of strong friends and 21 pairs of weak friends. There was a tendency for strong friends to play more constructively than weak friends.

Stemming from research on the determinants of creativity is a series of findings which relate satisfaction with key relationships to creative output. Perhaps, like the psychotherapy results, satisfying relationships help to release a person's desire to create. Baumgartel (1957) compared the self-reports of effectiveness by researchers working under democratic, autocratic, and laissex-faire supervisors. The scientists reported that they made more use of their present abilities, had greater freedom for originality, and made a higher contribution to basic science under democratic rather than authoritarian supervision. Andrews (1962) used more objective measures of creative performance—peer ratings, number of published reports, and output of patents—in an extensive study of scientific productivity. Research output was highest among men who were both high in self-determination and in communication with their supervisors. Drevdahl's (1965) study of creative psychologists showed similar results. Psychologists who were judged most creative by their colleagues recalled that their graduate programs were less authoritarian with less influence by their professors to go in the direction of the mentor's work and more influence on the selection of their research areas and formal courses. Each of the research climate studies was correlational, and the results do not rule out the possibility that the people who wanted to be creative were given more freedom, either because they asked for it or because it became apparent to their superior that this was a more effective way to operate.

Research findings from monkeys in a laboratory, children at play, patients in psychotherapy, and scientists in pursuit of creative solutions are consistent with the proposition that satisfaction of relatedness needs tends to increase desires for growth.

Growth Frustration and Relatedness Desires In their study of men on the assembly-line, Walker and Guest (1952) inquired of their 180 subjects whether the opportunity to talk with others was a reason for liking or not liking their jobs. One hundred thirty-seven of the men indicated that the chance to talk and joke with others was one reason, though not necessarily the main one, for liking their jobs. Some typical comments reported by Walker and Guest were:

> Talking with others takes up the strain of the job. It relieves the tension.
> Talking makes the time go faster.
> I like to talk because it breaks the monotony.
> If I couldn't talk to somebody, I'd be talking to myself.
> If it weren't for talking and fooling, you'd go nuts.

Even though these investigators provide no data from a group of people not working on assembly-line jobs, it seems reasonable to suggest that seeking social contact with fellow workers had a "driven" quality and that one aspect of the drive was to find relief from the monotony of their tasks.

The study by Wright (1943) mentioned above also contained data relevant to the relationship between growth frustration and relatedness desires. Behavior of the children was observed and coded during both the free play and the restricted play sessions. Cooperative behavior, defined as actively helping each other toward a common goal, showed a significant increase from the unrestricted to the frustrated play condition. Conflict behavior, measured by acts of aggression between children, decreased significantly from the first session to the second. Other kinds of behavior—watching each other, merely maintaining social contact, and impersonal interactions—showed no change between sessions. When the behavior changes were broken down into those between strong friends and those between weak friends, the overall significant change held for the strong friends, whereas only a trend showed for the weak friends.

There was a problem with this study because no control group of children having the complete set of toys for two sessions was observed. Perhaps the children got on with each other better simply because they had been together longer. Nevertheless, there were control observations showing that two kinds of behavior involving expressing more desires for relatedness needs increased, and three other kinds of behavior did not show noticeable changes.

The results of these two studies provide a basis for the proposition that frustrating growth needs tends to increase relatedness desires.

Relatedness Frustration and Existence Desires Revans (1964) completed a study of the training of student nurses in England. In three different hospitals researchers carried out a series of nondirective interviews with all the staff members: administrative nurses, trained nurses, untrained nurses, orderlies, lab technicians, and secretaries. A summary of the content analysis of the number of comments made by various jobs holders was presented by Revans. One of the content categories was "interpersonal relations." Revans remarked in the text that this category reflected difficulties with interpersonal relations. Five categories in the content analysis dealt with what the theory would term existence needs: Hours, food, supplies, pay, and working conditions. In a re-analysis of Revan's data (taken from Table 18, pp. 58–60), the present writer found that when the three hospitals were ordered according to their frustration with interpersonal relations, the average number of comments about existence needs (which could be termed expressing desires for

existence needs) tended to follow the same order.   Table 3-1 shows
the mean number of comments for each of the hospitals.

**Table 3-1.   Desire for Existence Needs when Relatedness Needs are
Frustrated**

Hospitals ordered by frustrated interpersonal relations	High	Medium	Low
Mean number of comments about existence needs	3.55	2.62	2.33

$$F_{2,15} = 3.26, p < .06, N = 6 \text{ jobs}$$

Jezernik (1968) found that the importance given to wages was
inversely correlated with being satisfied with supervision.   His interpretation of these findings was that the workers blamed the supervisors for poor pay.   Another interpretation could be that the
workers sought more pay to compensate for poor relations with
supervision.

Seashore and Bowers (1963) have reported the results of a field
experiment designed to assess the effects of instituting Likert's (1961)
theory of management.   Change agents from the University of
Michigan entered the organization with the purpose of helping the
members by (1) increasing the emphasis on the work group as a
functioning unit, (2) increasing supervisory support, (3) increasing
participation in decision-making, and (4) increasing influence and
interaction among organization members.   Three experimental and
two control groups provided the basis for the experiment, although
people were not randomly assigned to conditions.   The interventions
may be seen as ways of increasing the satisfaction of relatedness
needs.   To a considerable degree, the experimental conditions had
their desired effect for data showed that the experimental groups
increased in the use of work groups, in supportive behavior by peers
and superiors, and in influence with superiors.   Other measures
showed that the experimental groups became significantly more
satisfied with pay, working conditions, and security, while the control
groups showed no changes on these variables.   If it is reasonable to
assume that there were no actual changes between the groups on the
existence dimensions, then one might suggest that existence needs
became more satisfied because they were desired less, and they

were desired less because relatedness needs were better satisfied.

Research undertaken in a number of different organizational settings provides support for the proposition that frustration of relatedness needs is associated with increased existence desires. Generally speaking we have been able to show support and convergence for the E.R.G. need concepts and for the propositions showing desire as a function of satisfaction. But to find some support and some convergence is not to say that it is equally strong for all parts of the theory. Some parts are much better supported by known existing studies than others. The case for the innate quality and properties of the three needs can be made strongly from empirical evidence. The proposition associating growth desires to relatedness satisfaction and the one relating existence desires to relatedness frustration both had several studies from rather different orientations backing them. But the proposition tying relatedness desires to existence satisfaction had only one study behind it. The one associating relatedness desires to growth frustration was prompted by two investigations but neither was very rigorous or direct in the measurement of relatedness desires.

Satisfaction as a Function of Desires

Existence Needs Locke (1969) asked thirty white collar employees from a research firm to indicate their minimum adequate pay given their present needs and to indicate their anticipated satisfaction with 50 per cent less, 25 per cent less, the amount indicated, 25 per cent more, and 50 per cent more. The results showed an essentially linear function with anticipated satisfaction increasing with increased income.

Zaleznik and Moment (1964) asked executives who were attending a management development program to give their annual salary plus bonus, their preference for economic rewards, and their satisfaction. To analyze these data they divided the income groupings into three categories: below $20,000, above $30,000, and between $20,000 and 30,000. In each salary category, those with lower preferences for economic rewards reported greater satisfaction.

Relatedness Needs Kahn *et al.* (1964) studied the reactions of fifty-three managers to differing degrees of role conflict as a function of whether the men were introverts or extroverts. Extroverts prefer being with people in open and outgoing ways, while introverts prefer to be alone and solitary. One of the reactions which these investigators obtained from the managers was their degree of perceived trust with the people who were their role senders. Under conditions of low role conflict, the introverts tended to perceive slightly more trust than the extroverts. But under conditions of high role conflict, the extroverts tended to perceive greater trust. Their findings also showed that extroverts tended to communicate more frequently than introverts regardless of the conflict conditions. The overall pattern of these results suggests that the extroverts may perceive greater trust when their relationships are strained because they put more into the relationships at these times.

Growth Needs Hackman and Lawler (1971) studied the job characteristics, need intensity, and need satisfaction among hourly workers in a public utility corporation. Among employees with high needs for self-actualization, there was a positive correlation between variety and autonomy in their jobs and satisfaction with opportunities to use their skills and abilities. Among employees with low needs for self-actualization, there was essentially no correlation between variety and autonomy in their jobs and satisfaction of self-actualization needs.

Studies relevant to the impact of chronic existence, relatedness, and growth needs on the respective satisfactions were generally supportive of propositions 8 to 10 advanced by E.R.G. theory. In the case of existence needs there was support for $P8$ by both the Locke (1969) and Zaleznik and Moment (1964) studies. The data bearing on chronic relatedness needs were not as decisive because they did not exactly measure the relatedness concepts. However, to the extent that the results can be generalized, the Kahn *et al.* (1964) results do support $P9c$. In the case of growth needs, the Hackman and Lawler (1971) results support $P10$.

MASLOW'S THEORY

Maslow's (1943, 1954) theory of motivation has had a major influence on the thinking and research of many writers in the field of organizational behavior. In Argyris' (1964) work on the conflict between the individual and the organization, the concept of self-actualization played a central role. McGregor's (1960) formulation of the now famous managerial styles, theory *X* and theory *Y*, relied heavily on the idea that human motives were arranged in a hierarchy of prepotency. Porter (1962, 1963) based his national survey of managerial job attitudes on Maslow's conceptualizations, and later Haire, Ghiselli, and Porter (1966) did an international survey using Porter's measures of Maslow's needs. Beer (1966) also utilized Maslow's concepts for his empirical work on the relationship among employee needs, leadership, and motivation.

In addition, several writers have proposed modifications of Maslow's (1943, 1954) original framework. One such modification was suggested (though not explicitly stated as such) by Maslow (1962) himself when he wrote about deficiency and growth motivations. Barnes (1960) proposed a two-step hierarchy consisting of physiological needs at the base and a higher level made up of self-esteem, esteem of others, and belongingness. Harrison (1966) also offered a modification consisting of two levels, similar to that of Barnes. In his model, physiological-economic needs were at the base. Upon satisfaction of these needs, then a higher level of social *or* ego needs would be sought.

Clark (1960) produced a review of the literature organized around Maslow's original hierarchy. In that paper, he pointed out the need for a direct empirical test of Maslow's theory. However, until the recent work by Hall and Nougaim (1968) and Goodman (1968) that theory has not been tested directly in empirical research known to this writer.

Empirical Studies

Hall and Nougaim (1968) designed a longitudinal study to test key propositions in the Maslow theory. Using five annual interviews from each of 49 managers in A.T.&T., they developed operational definitions to test Maslow's predictions by both static and change analyses. Their results provide almost no support for Maslow's theory, with one exception. They did find a tendency among the higher-order needs for the satisfaction of a need to correlate with need intensity. Maslow's (1943) original statement of his theory did not discuss the consequences of self-actualization satisfaction. But in a later paper, he did say, "Growth is instead a continued, more or less steady upward and forward development. The more one gets, the more one wants, so that this kind of wanting is endless and can never be attained or satisfied" (1962, p. 31). In this instance, Hall and Nougaim's (1968) results provide support for Maslow's later formulation, and at the same time they also support the E.R.G. formulation concerning growth needs.

In another study of the Maslow theory, Goodman (1968) investigated the relative dominance of the three needs in the middle categories of the Maslow system—security, social, and ego. His study was conducted in a middle-sized electronics firm where nonsupervisory engineers and assembly-line workers served as subjects. From the fourteen assembly-line workers, only two showed a dominant motivation. Only seven of the twenty-four engineers showed a dominant motivation. For these cases of domination, six showed ego needs dominating social needs, and three showed security needs dominating social needs. From these results, Goodman said that there is a tendency for the security motive to be somewhere between the social and ego motives. He concludes that the Maslow hierarchy should not be considered a hierarchy in the particular situation.

Studies which offer direct tests of Maslow's theory are few in number and a mixed bag in terms of the kinds of conclusions that they offer. A case could be made that the theory has not really been tested. Hall and Nougaim (1968) reported that they had trouble developing operational definitions and reliable coding procedures in their study. Nevertheless, they did find positive correlations between satisfaction and desire for higher order needs. Goodman's (1968) study faces similar questions of a more severe nature because he showed no empirical data for the validity of his measures.

More recently, factor analytic studies by Payne (1970) and by Roberts, Walter, and Mills (1970) applied to the Porter scales have failed to show convergence among items designed to measure human needs as conceptualized by Maslow. This writer's conclusion would be that Maslow's theory is strongest conceptually and has received some empirical support in the area of self-actualization, but it is unclear and has little direct empirical support in other need areas.

Summary and Implications This chapter reported the empirical studies, other than those undertaken by the author, which might bear on the plausibility of the E.R.G. theory and the alternative models. Different degrees of support were found for various aspects of E.R.G. theory. The evidence which supported the three-fold need conceptualization came from many sources. Several E.R.G. propositions received wide support, while other propositions received some, but less extensive, support.

Extensive support was found for the simple frustration hypothesis, but there were also many studies which indicated that by itself, this proposition was not adequate to explain and predict the complex relationships between need satisfactions and desires. Data bearing on Maslow's theory strongly suggested that this conceptual scheme had difficulties with the middle level (interpersonal) needs. Whatever support for the theory that was found pertained to self-actualization needs. No support was found for predictions bearing on safety, belongingness and esteem needs.

From this review one could argue on empirical grounds that we are in need of a better approach to human needs than currently exists; that E.R.G. theory is strong where the alternative views are not; and that E.R.G. theory is also strong where the alternative approaches predict effectively.

Chapter 4

METHODS

RESEARCH in field settings offers the promise of greater realism at the cost of some imprecision with respect to the conclusions one may draw, especially with respect to causality. Empirical data for testing predictions from E.R.G. theory were collected from a number of different field settings by the use of questionnaires. The purpose of the present chapter is to describe the various field settings where data were gathered and the rationale for their selection and to explain the design of the questionnaires used to collect the data.

The field settings were not chosen haphazardly but were selected because each one had something to recommend its particular utility for testing certain aspects of the theory. In no small degree, the latter field settings were selected because earlier studies had pointed out that no single setting offered quite all the qualities that seemed necessary to pin down various leads which the initial studies seemed to suggest. As an experimenter might seek to design a new experiment after he learned the results of initial studies, we sought out field settings which offered new twists in terms of the kind and quality of need satisfactions they offered.

For a measuring instrument to be useful in theoretically oriented research, it should be tied to the concepts it seeks to investigate and relatively free from artifactual qualities which would needlessly cloud the conclusions one might draw from data. Sometimes these two characteristics may be at odds with each other. Tactics which might produce a quantitatively rigorous instrument can be so onerous to respondents that the data which are produced have many unknown sources of random and systematic error. Methods which might be easy for respondents to tolerate can produce data which are so loose and ill-structured that they are very difficult (if not impossible) to analyze systematically. There is art as well as science to instrument construction. An instrument must reflect an implicit theory. An instrument designed for theoretically oriented research has greater utility for others than its designer if the major links between concepts and concrete operations can be spelled out. For this research, the questionnaires were developed after considerable work with interviews and after a critical look at the instruments which had been based on Maslow's concepts.

FIELD SETTINGS

Characteristics

The settings utilized for data collection in this research consisted of:

(1) A medium-sized manufacturing firm, to be referred to as *Manufacturing*
(2) A medium-sized bank, to be referred to as *Bank*
(3) Two college fraternities from an eastern university, to be called *Alpha* and *Beta* Houses
(4) A boys preparatory school, to be termed *Boys School*
(5) A one-week human relations sensitivity training laboratory for adult members of the helping professions, to be called *Adult Lab*
(6) A two-day human relations sensitivity training laboratory for adolescents, to be referred to as *Adolescent Lab*
(7) A series of recruitment interviews for M.B.A. students seeking summer and permanent jobs, to be called *Recruitment Interviews.*

These quite different settings offered variation in subject populations and in the quality of need satisfaction obtainable. The period of data collection ran from the summer of 1965 to the fall of 1969, and the number of respondents in each organization ranged from about 50 to over 200. Table 4-1 provides the details for each setting.

Manufacturing was the largest division of a firm which produced innovative luxury products for a national market. Although relatively young, the firm had grown rapidly during the preceding ten years. Employing approximately 1,700 people in the manufacturing division at the time of the study, the company enjoyed a very favorable reputation in the local labor market. It was stated by some personnel people that they were able to employ a selection ratio of 1:10 for hourly employees. The president and other senior managers were highly committed to having a "meaningful work life" for employees. In addition to having a policy of above average pay and benefits, Manufacturing had developed a job-enlargement program for one department which had a continuous process assembly-line technology. Participants in this program were carefully selected from their already above average work force. They were given both general education (mathematics, English, physics, and chemistry) and training to be able to obtain the highly automated assembly-line equipment. Their jobs consisted of operating the equipment in teams of four and of dealing with various staff functions such as personnel, scheduling, and planning functions.

At the time of the study, the enlargement program was both a source of pride and of tension for the management. The entire project had been undertaken by the company staff without much (if any) aid from behavioral scientists. They were understandably uncomfortable with the idea that some researchers would be entering to second-guess their efforts. Prior to the entry of researchers, there were some overt signs of tension connected with the program. One manager who had been in charge of the department had resigned, and one of the staff members working with the program had had a serious heart attack. The research understanding reached with this department was that they would receive no more or no less attention in the study than other departments in Manufacturing.

Chris Argyris undertook a research-consulting project with the top ten managers in Manufacturing while this writer selected a random sample of employees and managers from all departments within the division. Approximately half of the respondents in the study were interviewed before they filled out questionnaires. After all of the data had been collected, a report was prepared, and the writer spent several months discussing the results with managers and their subordinates.

Located in an eastern urban setting, Bank was one of the three largest banks in a city of over 150,000 people. It had a main office and seventeen branches and employed approximately 750 people.

The organization had a history of participating in behavioral science studies of the organization. Approximately fifteen years earlier, Argyris (1954) had done a study of this organization and found that they had a tendency to select a certain "right type" of personality, who tended to prefer routine activities, distance in interpersonal relations, safe decisions, and the absence of aggression in the personalities of others. During the period after Argyris' (1954) study, Bank engaged in a number of activities whose outcome could have served to increase the dynamism of their management team. A number of mergers took place, bringing in managers from different organizational cultures. Several new services which drew employees from nonbanking financial institutions, such as finance companies, were begun. A training and selection program for younger managers was initiated. Persons selected for this program tended to be well-educated, initiative-taking, and outgoing in their relations with others, according to the personality test information utilized by Bank. While Bank was able to be quite selective in its choice of managers for the training program, it faced a sparse labor market in the choice of employees. Just prior to the time of the study, the cut-off score for clerical aptitude had been lowered. One personnel man indicated that the Bank was practically willing to take anyone who came in off the street.

Persons were selected at random to participate in the study, with the exception of the senior management where everyone participated. Approximately half of the participants were interviewed prior to taking a questionnaire. Some of the subjects participated in individual interviews and others in group interviews and were randomly assigned to group and individual interview conditions.

Bank was interested in having the study done to see if their organizational life had changed in significant ways from Argyris' earlier findings. At the conclusion of the study, two reports were prepared, one giving an overview of the entire organization and the other focussing specifically on the management development program. Several months were spent with bank managers going over the reports.

There were a number of ways that Manufacturing and Bank provided complementary samples. The work force in Manufacturing was predominantly blue collar, while it was mainly white collar in Bank. Manufacturing was able to be far more selective in its choice of employees than Bank could be. Finally, the proportion of managers who were educated in modern methods of management was much higher in Manufacturing than Bank. The idea that organizations could be redesigned to make them more responsive to human concerns was much more widely accepted in Manufacturing than it was in Bank.

Both Manufacturing and Bank were primarily economically oriented systems, however. Their prime purpose was to make money. The extent to which they could afford to devote attention to the human needs of their employees always took second place to their primary aims of achieving a profit and a high rate of return on the investment of capital. Educational institutions, on the other hand, give their primary allegiance to the growth and development of their members. Economic constraints exist but in the service of other human needs, not prior to them.

The opportunity to study college fraternities came when, as a result of a course in organizational behavior given by Thomas Lodahl and myself, one of the members of Alpha House asked whether we would conduct some laboratory (T-group) training for their organization. We responded that when laboratory methods were responsibly applied to living systems, an organizational diagnosis of the house should precede decisions about how laboratory methods might be applied. The members, in an open meeting, agreed to participate in the study after questioning us very thoroughly about our commitment to help them and about the confidentiality of the data we would obtain.

Beta House was approached by the investigators shortly after the data from the first fraternity was obtained. One of the graduate assistants in the organizational behavior course had expressed interest in our work with Alpha House (without knowing which house it was), so we asked whether he thought his house would be interested in participating in the study. After he took up the matter with the brothers, we were invited to eat some meals at the house. During these meals we had an opportunity to meet many of the brothers and to interview them informally about life in their fraternity. After these initial sessions, we attended a house meeting to explain the project in more detail. Very few questions were asked by the brothers, who quickly and easily agreed to participate.

The questionnaire administered in Beta House was identical to that used in Alpha House. After the data had been collected, a report summarizing the results was prepared, including comparative data with Alpha House, and given to Beta House. Beta House showed no interest in further exploration or consultation.

E.R.G. theory is basically a dynamic theory concerned with changes in satisfactions and desires. Each of the organizations described above provided an opportunity to obtain cross sectional or static data to test derivations from the theory but none offered the possibility of getting time-series data. Longitudinal data are quite expensive to obtain due to time demands, loss of subjects, and the investment required of organization members. The two settings to be discussed next provided an opportunity to obtain longitudinal data because respondents were willing to make the additional investment needed to complete the questionnaires more than once, perhaps because they felt they might have something to gain from doing so. Nevertheless the response rate in both settings was about 50 per cent for those people who provided complete data at each administration. This contrasts markedly with the static response rates which ran above 85 per cent on the average.

Work with Boys School grew out of the school's reaction to a two-day laboratory education program which had been conducted for their seniors and girls from a neighboring boarding school. As a result of the laboratory education program, key members of the faculty became interested in the utilization of behavioral science for the improvement and enrichment of the organization's human qualities. David Brown and the writer began a year-long diagnostic study of the system which included the collection of some longitudinal data on E.R.G. satisfactions and desires. Measures of chronic needs and satisfactions were obtained from students before school began in September and then again mid-way through the fall term in November. Thus the time spread between measures was approximately $2\frac{1}{2}$ months.

This study included individual and group interviews with organization members and resulted in a report on the system. Included in the report were an analysis of the system's impact on students and faculty and some action steps which might be undertaken to enable the school to deal with its problems more effectively. At the time of this writing, the school was in the process of acting on the recommendations.

Adult Lab was conducted by the State of Michigan Training Laboratories for a population of persons engaged in the helping professions of teaching, the ministry, and social work. There were seven T-groups in the laboratory. One of them was for alumni; the rest were persons participating in their first training experience. Sessions were conducted from Saturday through Saturday, and the questionnaires measuring satisfactions and instantaneous desires were administered on Sunday, Wednesday, and Friday. In this case, the time spread between administrations of the questionnaire was only a matter of days. Feedback on the Sunday and Wednesday results was provided to the participants just after they had completed the Friday administration.

Each of the preceding studies was designed primarily to investigate how satisfaction affected desire, but the remaining two studies were concerned with whether persons with varying chronic desires obtained differential satisfactions when they were exposed to similar situations.

Adolescent Lab was a two-day laboratory conducted in a special program for seniors and faculty at neighboring boys' and girls' boarding schools. Participants were randomly assigned to T-groups so that there would be two student-faculty, three boy-girl, and three all-boy groups. Two weeks prior to conducting the laboratories a meeting was held with all of the potential participants at which the nature of the laboratory was explained. At the conclusion of the explanation and a question and answer session, the people were asked to complete the E.R.G. chronic needs scale. Half-way through the laboratory, they were asked to complete a questionnaire to register their need satisfactions from the laboratory.

These data were used in an evaluation of the laboratory that was presented to the faculty and administration of the boys' school.

The study of Recruitment Interviews was concerned with the degree to which M.B.A. students of varying chronic relatedness needs obtained satisfaction from job interviews. Approximately half of the students in the sample were first-year students looking for summer jobs, while the other half were second-year students in search of permanent jobs. Near the end of the recruitment period, the students were asked to complete a questionnaire containing an E.R.G. chronic needs measure and satisfaction scales pertaining to their best, average, and worst interviews. Feedback from this study was provided to all students who wished it.

Key Variables

The organizational settings which have been described here differ from each other in ways that were important with respect to a number of theoretical considerations. In each setting, it was necessary to decide which satisfactions and desires to measure. The primary criterion for making this decision was whether it seemed as though particular issues would be viewed as meaningful and legitimate by organization members. Informal discussions between the researcher and organization members were used to test out various possibilities and to invite participants to contribute their suggestions of meaningful topics.

Bank offered a number of possibilities which Manufacturing did not provide, for example. One of the major ways in which these two types of organizations differed from each other was that most Bank employees dealt with customers while Manufacturing employees did not. Therefore, there were significant others in their work lives who were not members of their primary work group. Questions about customer relationship satisfactions and desires were included in the Bank study only while participants in both studies were asked satisfaction and desire questions about their supervisors and coworkers. It was also learned from Bank members that many worried about their physical safety because of occasional robberies. In the Bank study, satisfaction and desire questions about physical harm were included while they were not in the Manufacturing study. Pay and fringe benefits were studied in both business organizations.

The fraternities offered the possibility of settings where more than one ecological setting was relevant to the respondents. All of the fraternity members spent substantial portions of their time in both house activities and in academic work. Consequently, in this setting it was possible to measure growth variables with respect to more than one environment, while in the business organizations the job was the only relevant and legitimate environment.

As will become more apparent in Chapter 7, the complexities

which surround understanding the operation of relatedness satisfactions and desires are probably greater than for the other needs. All laboratory education settings offered the possibility of measuring a higher quality of relatedness satisfaction than is usually observed in normal organization settings. The fraternities also offered settings with interesting qualities for measuring relatedness satisfaction. These organizations were formed with the explicit purpose of establishing a climate which fostered brotherhood among members.

Informal conversations with M.B.A. job candidates revealed that most of them faced recruitment interviews of quite variable satisfaction. For men in the process of beginning their careers as professional managers, a job interview is a very important event. A good interview is a very satisfying experience, and a poor one is a depressing encounter.

Table 4-1   Organizational Settings with Dates and Sample Sizes

Setting	Date	Sample Size
Manufacturing	Summer, 1965	176
Bank	Fall, 1968	217
Alpha House	Spring, 1968	57
Beta House	Spring, 1968	46
Boys' School	Fall, 1969	77
Adult Lab	Spring, 1968	46
Adolescent Lab	Spring, 1969	83
Recruitment Interviews	Spring, 1967	112

INSTRUMENTS

Maslow Categories

At the time when research on E.R.G. theory began, there were two instruments available for measuring Maslow's needs from the empirical literature. The first questionnaire was developed by Lyman Porter for his national survey on managerial job attitudes (Porter, 1962; 1963). His instrument consisted of sixteen items which he called "characteristics or qualities connected with your own management position" in the questionnaire. These items were precoded according to security, social, esteem, autonomy, and self-actualization needs based on Maslow's theory. The format for these items was for each respondent to answer three questions, each on a seven-point scale, for each quality or characteristic. A sample item was:

The opportunity for personal growth and development in my management position.

(a) How much is there now? (min) 1 2 3 4 5 6 7 (max)
(b) How much should there be? 1 2 3 4 5 6 7
(c) How important is this to me? 1 2 3 4 5 6 7

Porter's instrument contains 15 such items in addition to one for pay, which he did not consider to be one of Maslow's needs. Porter used the answer to question (a) as a measure of need fulfillment and the difference between (b) and (a) as a measure of need dissatisfaction.

Porter did not use his instrument to test Maslow's theory but to study the relationship of need fulfillment, dissatisfaction, and importance to various organizational variables such as position, size, and tallness-flatness. If this instrument were to be used to test Maslow's theory, there would be a serious problem of response bias to be handled. A person filling out this instrument gives his fulfillment and importance ratings almost simultaneously, where the items for both variables are identical. Thus, a respondent could easily produce correlated responses between fulfillment and importance for a given item because the ratings were produced contemporaneously on scales with identical directions.

The data produced from this response bias problem would not necessarily support predictions from Maslow's theory. It is not altogether clear how these methodological problems would affect the outcome of Maslow's predictions. Perhaps they would favor finding positive relationships between fulfillment and desires for all variables. Perhaps they would only increase the error of measurement, thereby reducing the likelihood of finding any relationships.

Another approach to the measurement of Maslow needs has been developed by Beer (1966). While he escaped to some degree the problem of developing artifactual correlations between fulfillment and importance, his method was characterized by a different methodological problem. He used precoded items for the same five need categories employed by Porter. The format of his presentation of items was different, however. There were separate parts of his questionnaire for getting importance and fulfillment data.

A "Preference Inventory" provided respondents with five item sets of "Job factors" which they were asked to rank in order of their importance. Each set had one precoded item representing one of the Maslow need categories. In another part of the questionnaire, respondents were asked to complete a "Job Inventory" consisting of five-item sets of "things you can get from your job." Again each set contained one precoded item from each of the Maslow need categories. Respondents were again asked to rank the items within each set, this time according to the order that "they reflect things you are getting from your job." A sample set from the Job Inventory was:

——— There is an opportunity to develop my full potential on the job.
——— I am told what I am supposed to do and how I am to do it.
——— There is relative freedom from supervision.
——— My job gives me status.
——— There is an opportunity to develop close friendships in my job.

Subjects faced six sets of items similar to these, all of which had been equated for social desirability. Beer developed subscale total scores by adding the ranks assigned to the items in each need category. This procedure, while free of the methodological problems noted for the Porter scales, has its own problem of forcing negative correlations among the need scales. The procedure does not provide methodologically independent measures of the different need fulfillments and preferences. Beer (1966, p. 27) noted this problem. He did not report results which would have served to test Maslow's theory.

One can only speculate about the way in which this methodological problem would affect tests of Maslow's theory. Perhaps the forced negative correlations would result in positive correlations between fulfillment and preferred measures. Perhaps the artifact would only add to the error variance on both measures.

Informally, this writer learned that Schneider had developed an instrument to operationalize Maslow satisfactions. Schneider had developed his instrument independently of knowing about E.R.G. theory and was willing to share his method and results with this writer. In developing his scales, he asked students to read Maslow's theory and Douglas McGregor's (1960) account of it. From these conceptual inputs, a large set of items were prepared. Then eight graduate students were asked to sort the items into the categories of security, social, esteem, autonomy, and self-actualization needs.

Each item was rated on a seven-point scale on how well it applied to the category in which it was placed.   Only those items which received a rating of 6 or more by all raters were retained for the questionnaire. Schneider prepared eight sets of five items and used the following instructions.

On the following pages of Part III are presented eight sets of statements about things you do in your position as a nurse.   Each set has five alternatives which can be responded to on the same scale.   You are to decide how appropriate *each* of the alternatives in a given set is, on the basis of your general feelings about your position as a nurse, and indicate your decision by placing the letter representing the alternative on the 15-point scale immediately below the set.

A BRIEF EXAMPLE:

> I do things:
>   (*a*) that are fun.
>   (*b*) to earn a lot of money.

```
:        b :            :          :          : a            :
:   :   :   :   :   :   :   :   :   :   :   :   :   :   :   :
```

```
:        :            :          :   :      :            :
Not at all          Moderately          Very True
   True                True
```

First complete the statement using alternative "a."   If you feel that your nursing position is generally fun you would place the letter "*a*" as it is placed in the sample above.   Now complete the statement using alternative "*b*."   If you feel you do not do things to earn a lot of money, you should place the letter "*b*" somewhere near where it has been placed in the sample scale.

You are to evaluate each of the following sets of alternatives in the same way.   Please be sure to evaluate *all* five alternatives, *a, b, c, d,* and *e,* for each set.   Although you are allowed to place two alternatives for a given set in the same subdivision of the line, you should not do so unless it is absolutely impossible for you to differentiate between them.

This procedure had the advantage of being tied to theoretical concepts urging respondents to discriminate among degrees of satisfaction for different needs, and yet not being as prone to forcing negative correlations as Beer's procedure.   Items developed by Schneider were used in the current research and will be discussed in more detail in subsequent chapters.

E.R.G. Categories

The procedure for developing satisfaction and desire measures for E.R.G. variables was intended to avoid both of the major pitfalls of the Porter and Beer procedures. The goal was to minimize response bias and provide for methodologically independent measures for each satisfaction and desire scale. To do this, a number of procedures were followed. Satisfaction measures were made in one part of the questionnaire and desire measures in another. A different format was used for the two types of measures.

Satisfaction Measures Satisfaction items appeared in a six-point agree-disagree Likert scale format. Some of the items were phrased such that agreement would represent need satisfaction while others were written so that disagreement would represent need satisfaction.

For example:

In my job, I am often bored. (Agreement would represent dissatisfaction with growth.)
It's easy to talk with my boss about my job. (Agreement would represent satisfaction with respect from superiors.)

There were approximately the same number of positively and negatively worded items in each satisfaction scale.

The content of specific items evolved out of a dialectic process between theoretical considerations and empirical reality. On the one hand, it was necessary to develop items which were linked to E.R.G. concepts. On the other hand, little was accomplished if the theoretical basis for the items was abundantly clear to professional investigators but lacked meaning for the persons who would respond to the questions. A key heuristic that was employed in item construction was to attempt to develop items which were *descriptive* of *subjective* states. To the extent that this goal could be achieved, respondents would be discouraged from giving the socially acceptable answer and yet they would find it easy to give an account of their need satisfaction. Items with these qualities were developed from listening to answers which respondents gave to open-enedd interview questions. The prototypic interview answer would consist of a respondent saying that he was satisfied, displeased, happy, or unhappy with a particular condition which he would describe. If the condition was a relatively pure case of one of the E.R.G. needs, then the descriptive account would be abstracted to make a questionnaier item. For example, an interview response was:

> Well, personally, I'm satisfied as long as I can learn new things. And, like I said before, down here there's not that much more I can learn. Whereas if I were learning something, the time would go by much quicker. I know I'd be happier.

The growth satisfaction item from such an account would be:

> I seldom get the feeling of learning new things from my work.

Relatedness satisfaction deserves special attention in terms of item development both because of the difference with Maslow's theory and because respondents were often reluctant to say negative things about their relationships. After some experience in listening one could develop a sense of the ways people would use to cover troublesome relationships. For example, a person talking about his peer group relationships said:

> I think it's good. I know I am able to talk to any of them and not have any animosity or bad feelings.

From such an account one might readily infer that the respondent was trying to keep negative feelings from being present in the relationship. In spite of this, he said that the relationship was good. Events such as this support a general avoidance of evaluations in assessing the satisfaction obtained from relationships because there also can be times when a direct evaluation does seem consistent with the nature of the relationship. A person discussing his relationship with his boss said:

> When we get through talking, I would see his side of it and he would see mine, but we would do it one way and both of us agree that's the way it should be done. We never walk out, saying I still think you're wrong. Very rarely. We come to an understanding. I can talk to him. He's willing to change his mind. And I'm willing to change my mind. This mutual respect for each other adds to the good relationship we have.

From this account, one gets a very clear sense of mutuality in the relationship. Both positive and negative feelings were discussed. Influence was mutual. They remained in contact even when the relationship became stressful. When, after these descriptions, a

positive evaluation is given one can have more confidence in its
validity. It would therefore make sense to take a statement made in
such a context as indicative of relatedness satisfaction to a subordinate from a superior. A relatedness satisfaction item taken from
such an account could be:

It's easy to talk with my boss about my job.

Episodic Desire Measures Desire items appeared in a different
format in a different part of the questionnaire with different wording
than satisfaction items for the same need categories. Each item was
rated for importance and desire on five-point scales where 1 = not
important, 5 = extremely important; 1 = no more, 5 = very much
more. For example:

Openness and honesty between my boss and me
———— Importance
———— Desire
Being challenged by my work
———— Importance
———— Desire

Each need had several items to form its desire scale, and there were
two ratings for each item. The purpose of the multiple ratings was
to provide a way to increase the reliability of the desire scales. In
each case, the "more" ratings were considered to be the prime
measure of desire with added reliability being provided by the
"importance" ratings. As we shall see in the next chapter, it was not
always feasible to use the "importance" ratings because they did not
correlate with the "more" ratings for all need areas.

Chronic Desire Measures The instrument used to measure
chronic needs had to be both short and reliable for the kinds of uses
to which it was put. Often reliability can be increased by adding
length but this luxury was not useful for the current studies. It took
some experimenting to develop an instrument with these qualities.
An assumption was added in this case which had been carefully
avoided in the preceding E.R.G. instruments. For this instrument,
we were willing to ask respondents to use a limited force-choice
format. A list of factors was developed which included specific
E.R.G. items and some nontheoretically oriented items. Each
respondent was asked to give a priority ranking to the items and to

distribute 100 points among the factors. In the case of chronic needs, the forced choice format was reasonable because in the course of his overall activities no person has limitless time. He must make choices (perhaps not always with full awareness) about how he will invest himself. The chronic needs questionnaire simply asked him to register these general preferences.

Some General Issues

Items for testing E.R.G. theory were generally formed to apply across organizational settings. At the same time, however, an effort was made to write items which were empathic to the needs and issues for people in the various settings. Consequently, the instruments were modified slightly depending on the settings in which they were used. Only in the two fraternities were exactly identical instruments used. If there is convergence of findings across settings, then the fact that items can be rewritten to fit idiosyncratic qualities of the settings increases one's confidence in the theory underlying the item construction. An instrument containing all three types of measures in the way they were presented to respondents in Bank is shown in Appendix A.

Several studies in the series employed static correlations between measures taken from the satisfaction portion of the questionnaire and measures taken from the desire portion of the questionnaire. Even if the procedures described above worked in the ways intended, there remains the possibility that certain correlations might be obtained as a result of a respondent's attempt to appear consistent in his own eyes or in the eyes of others. Such a person might develop his "theory" about what goes together and give his answers accordingly. Unless his theory was identical to E.R.G. theory, this approach should work against finding support for some E.R.G. predictions and in favor of others. One likely respondent theory might be that anything that he finds inadequate is also something to desire more. A person answering the questions from this perspective might produce the expected *negative* correlation between pay satisfaction and desire but would not produce the predicted *positive* correlation between growth satisfaction and desire. In short, while the operation of a respondent's desire to be consistent might artifactually produce one set of supportive results for the theory, it might work against others. We should observe the pattern of results in the later chapters to see if such a methodological artifact is a viable hypothesis for explaining the results which are obtained.

Summary The present research was a series of correlational studies carried out in diverse organizational settings with the collaboration of the organization members. The settings offered varying populations of respondents and differed from each other in terms of their relevance for testing various aspects of E.R.G. theory. Three general types of instruments were employed to measure E.R.G. variables. Separate formats were developed for satisfaction, episodic desire, and chronic desire. These formats were designed to avoid specific methodological pitfalls and present an instrument which respondents could meaningfully answer.

Chapter 5

EMPIRICAL VALIDITY

THE first step in testing hypotheses from a theory is to see whether the variables defined conceptually can be measured operationally. One would wish to know whether efforts to measure the same variable converge with each other more than they do with efforts to measure different variables. This is the question of convergent and discriminant validity which Campbell and Fiske (1959) have defined. Another empirical question is whether measures of theoretically defined variables correlate in expected ways with other variables external to the particular theoretical system. We have used the term "predictive validity" to cover this issue. Issues concerning how variables within the theory relate to each other empirically will be the subject of subsequent chapters.

CONVERGENT VALIDITY

The Bank study was a principal one on a number of validity questions. In this study, both E.R.G. items and Maslow items, as they had been developed by Schneider, were answered by respondents. In the same questionnaire, a number of other job-related attitudes (such as involvement and job satisfaction) were also measured. For the E.R.G. items, the factor analytic study was an attempt to replicate an earlier study (Alderfer, 1967) and extend it by predicting where new factors should appear if certain new items were written. For the Maslow items, it was an attempt to see if the items written from this theory showed a tendency to converge as the conceptualization would predict. There were more subjects in this study than in any other, and the range on many demographic variables, such as income, job level, sex, age, and seniority, was relatively wide. These factors would tend to produce variance in the measures, and the sample size would tend to produce relatively stable correlations. Each set of items was intercorrelated, factor analyzed by the principal components methods, and rotated according to the varimax procedure. All of the factors with eigen values greater than one were rotated and those factors accounting for the highest percentage of variance were reported.

E.R.G. Satisfaction Scales Most of the items in this study were identical or very similar to the ones used in the initial convergent validity report (Alderfer, 1967). In addition, items purporting to develop two new scales, safety from physical harm and respect from customers, were included. The first of these represents an additional existence need, while the second deals with a new relatedness need. Physical integrity of a person's body was the particular material end for the existence need, while customers were the significant others for the relatedness need.

Table 5-1 presents the results of factor analyzing the full set of satisfaction items. For ease of reading, all of the items concerning a specific need are presented together even though they were systematically spread throughout the questionnaire. All six of the items expected to form a pay satisfaction factor had loadings above .60 on a single factor, and there were no loadings on this factor above .24 from any other items nor did any of these items load above .20 on other factors. These items concerned both relative and absolute statements. All of the items that were expected to form a fringe benefits factor had loadings of .60 or higher on a single factor, and there were no loadings above .22 on this factor from other items nor did these items have loadings above .24 on other factors. The items expected to form a physical safety factor loaded on a single factor with weights of .78 or larger, showed no loadings above .18 on other factors, and had no loadings above .28 from other items.

Seven of the eight items expected to form a respect from superiors factor had loadings above .55 on a single factor, had no loadings above .28 on other factors, and had no other items loading above .34

with them. Three of the five items expected to form a respect from
peers factor had loadings above .53 on a single factor, had no loadings above .28 on other factors, and had no other items loading
above .28 with them. All four of the items expected to form a
respect from customers factor had loadings above .54 on a single
factor, had no loadings above .22 on other factors, and had no items
above .23 loading with them. From these results it would seem that
of the three significant others, coworkers are the least well defined.
In each case, however, the items which formed the factors included
ones indicating mutuality of both positive and negative exchanges.
On the superiors factor there were loadings on both credit for work
and need for improvement. On the peers factor, there were loadings
on providing help and on accepting differing opinions. For the
customers factor, there were loadings for receiving respect and
understanding and for being open.

All six of the items expected to form a growth factor had loadings
above .56 on a single factor, had no loadings above .26 on other
factors, and had no other items loading above .27 with them. The
content of these items included being utilized and learning from job
experiences. A person with high scores on this factor was not bored,
and he felt challenged in learningful ways.

Convergence between Questionnaire and Interview Measures
Campbell and Fiske's (1959) concepts of convergent and discriminant
validity apply more broadly than factor analysis alone and refer to
validity coefficients obtained between maximally different methods
used to measure the same traits. When measures of the same traits
obtained by maximally different methods correlate with each other,
there is evidence for convergent validity. Evidence for discriminant
validity is strengthened according to three criteria: (1) When the
correlation between two different measures of the same trait are
higher than correlations between two different traits where the
methods of measuring the different traits are different; (2) when the
correlations between two different measures of the same trait are
higher than correlations between two different traits where the method
of measuring the different traits is the same; and (3) when the pattern
of correlations among traits is common both within and among
methods.

In the Manufacturing study, satisfaction data were obtained

Table 5-1. E.R.G. Satisfaction Items Factor Analysis (Extended and Replicated) *

	Pay	Fringe benefits	Physical harm	Respect from superiors	Respect from peers	Respect from customers	Growth
Pay							
1. Compared to the rates for similar work here, my pay is good. (Agree)	.86	-.02	-.04	-.04	-.02	.05	.14
2. Compared to similar jobs in other places, my pay is poor. (Disagree)	.80	-.20	.03	-.11	.02	-.07	.09
3. I do not make enough money from my job to live comfortably. (Disagree)	.63	-.16	.01	-.11	.18	-.03	.27
4. Compared to the rates for less demanding jobs, my pay is poor. (Disagree)	.78	-.11	-.07	-.15	.03	-.08	.07
5. My pay is adequate to provide for the basic things in life. (Agree)	.64	-.06	-.02	-.08	.30	-.11	.06
6. Considering the work required, the pay for my job is what it should be. (Agree)	.79	-.09	-.11	-.12	.07	-.15	-.05
Fringe Benefits							
7. Our fringe benefits do not cover many of the areas they should. (Disagree)	-.15	.77	.07	-.04	.03	-.14	-.04
8. The fringe benefit program here gives nearly all the security I want. (Agree)	.16	.60	.18	-.19	.10	-.02	-.05
9. The fringe benefit program here needs improvement. (Disagree)	-.10	.85	.01	.09	.09	.10	.14
10. Compared to other places, our fringe benefits are excellent. (Agree)	-.24	.78	-.03	.14	.18	-.07	-.03

Physical Danger

11. I feel completely safe from physical harm in the work that I do. (Agree)	-.06	.11	.86	.03	-.18	.04	.04
12. I sense that my physical well-being is sometimes in danger in my work. (Disagree)	-.10	.01	.78	.14	.00	.16	.03

Respect from Superiors

13. My boss will play one person against another. (Disagree)	-.15	-.06	.28	.61	-.05	.22	-.11
14. My boss takes account of my wishes and desires. (Agree)	-.05	.04	.06	.75	-.13	-.34	-.09
15. My boss discourages people from making suggestions. (Disagree)	-.11	.09	.06	.70	.00	.03	-.08
16. It's easy to talk with my boss about my job. (Agree)	-.06	.05	.06	.79	-.12	.11	-.18
17. My boss does not let me know when I could improve my performance. (Disagree)	.00	.21	-.05	.58	-.04	.16	.10
18. My boss gives me credit when I do good work. (Agree)	-.20	-.02	.00	.75	-.19	-.05	-.08
19. My boss expects people to do things his way. (Disagree)	.10	.04	.03	(-.22)	.06	.00	.06
20. My boss keeps me informed about what is happening in the company. (Agree)	-.22	-.13	-.12	.51	-.21	.08	-.14

Table 5-1. (*continued*)

	Pay	Fringe benefits	Physical harm	Respect from superiors	Respect from peers	Respect from customers	Growth
Respect from Peers							
21. My coworkers are uncooperative unless it's to their advantage. (Disagree)	.21	.08	-.07	-.28	.53	-.19	.13
22. I can count on my coworkers to give me a hand when I need it. (Agree)	.10	-.07	-.10	-.28	.76	-.07	.13
23. I cannot speak my mind to my coworkers. (Disagree)	.16	.06	.10	-.19	.33	.01	.02
24. My coworkers welcome opinions different from their own. (Agree)	.13	.15	-.09	-.12	.63	.10	.20
25. My coworkers will not stick out their necks for me. (Disagree)	.13	-.01	-.04	.16	.36	.19	.07
Respect from Customers							
26. I find some customers extremely respectful of me. (Agree)	-.22	.05	-.08	.12	.01	.54	.07
27. I am unable to be very open with customers. (Disagree)	.10	-.07	.04	.11	.07	.81	-.12
28. I find some customers rarely understand my point of view. (Disagree)	-.04	.22	.19	.16	.00	.61	-.11
29. I find that I am really able to be myself with customers. (Agreed)	-.06	-.07	-.12	-.04	-.18	.59	-.06

Growth

30. I seldom get the feeling of learning new things from my work. (Disagree)	.08	.07	.19	.14	.06	-.22	.56
31. I have an opportunity to use many of my skills at work. (Agree)	.22	-.03	.02	-.23	-.03	-.07	.72
32. In my job, I am often bored. (Disagree)	-.08	-.05	-.07	-.01	.15	.17	.65
33. I use a wide range of abilities in my work. (Agree)	.16	.12	.08	-.08	.05	.09	.82
34. I make one or more important decisions every day. (Agree)	.05	-.06	-.06	.04	.26	-.26	.62
35. I do not have an opportunity to do challenging things at work. (Disagree)	.13	.20	.04	-.26	.10	.20	.61

* *Note:* Items underlined were expected to load on the specific factors while items in parentheses were not expected to have high loadings where they did.

Empirical Validity

through open-ended interview questions and by the fixed-alternative questionnaires. Even though these data have been reported elsewhere (Alderfer, 1967), a portion are repeated here in order to form a more complete picture of the convergent and discriminant validity of the satisfaction measures. All of the respondents who provided data by both methods were interviewed before they took the questionnaire. This order was followed because it seemed less likely that respondents would bias their questionnaire answers based on open-ended interview questions than vice versa.

Table 5-2. Satisfaction Scale Multitrait-Multimethod Matrix

	Questionnaire ($n = 302$)					*Interview*				
	P	**FB**	**RS**	**RP**	**G**	**P**	**FB**	**RS**	**RP**	**G**
Questionnaire										
P	(.88)									
FB	.00	(.80)								
RS	.01	.00	(.84)							
RP	−.02	.00	.00	(.79)						
G	−.01	.00	.02	−.04	(.88)					
			($n = 111$)					($n = 75$)		
Interview										
P	.54	.19	.15	−.18	.17	(.90)				
FB	.13	.47	.11	−.12	.09	.23	(.90)			
RS	.22	−.04	.66	−.13	.21	.19	.10	(.91)		
RP	.13	−.10	.14	.24	.15	.00	.07	.16	(.84)	
G	.19	.12	.02	.05	.61	.15	.11	.17	.10	(.87)

Note: The validity diagonal is indicated by the underlined coefficients; the reliability diagonals by the entries in parentheses.

Constraints of time and money did not allow all the interviews to be scored by both coders. The diagonals of the interview–interview submatrix are based on $n = 75$, the number of interviews done by both coders. All of the other interview cells are based on the coder who did all the interviews, $n = 111$.

Abbreviations: P = Pay; FB = Fringe Benefits; RS = Respect by Superiors; RP = Respect by Peers; G = Growth.

Table 5-2 presents the multitrait, multimethod matrix for these data. The results indicate that there were moderately high correlations between interview and questionnaire measures for the same satisfactions, thereby establishing some evidence for convergent validity. It can also be seen that the convergent validity coefficients both are higher than the correlations between different traits measured by different methods and higher than the correlations between different traits measured by the same method, thereby providing evidence meeting the first two criteria of discriminant validity. Evidence for the third criterion of discriminant validity is more ambiguous. If one were to observe only the questionnaire-questionnaire submatrix, he might conclude that the satisfaction variables are fully orthogonal. If one were to observe only the interview-interview submatrix, he might conclude that there were small but positive correlations among the variables. Since the entries in the questionnaire-questionnaire portion are based on factor scores from a principal components varimax factor analysis, they consist of data from a procedure designed to maximize orthogonality. The interview data suggest that there are positive correlations among various satisfactions and that these correlations tend to be higher between needs from a given category.

E.R.G. Episodic Desire Scales The Bank study was also designed to replicate and extend the factor analysis of E.R.G. desire scales. As with the satisfaction items, two new sets of items for physical harm and respect from customers were added to the items which had been studied earlier. The results of this analysis are shown in Table 5-3.

All four of the items expected to form a desire for pay factor had loadings above .61 on a single factor, had no loadings from other items above .38, and did not have loadings above .38 on other factors. Three of the four items expected to form a desire for fringe benefits factor had loadings above .63 on a single factor, but this factor also showed one item from the physical danger desires with a loading of .40 and one item from the set had a loading of .43 on another factor. All four of the items expected to form a desire to be safe from physical danger factor had loadings above .46 on a single factor and no loadings above .23 on other factors, but several of these items had loadings of .50 or greater on another factor. The "more" items expected to form three separated relatedness desire factors turned out to form a single factor. All of these items had loadings of .73 or higher on this factor and no loadings above .22 on other factors but there were four items from other items which also had loadings

Table 5-3. E.R.G. Desire Items Factor Analysis * (Extended and Replicated)

	Pay	Fringe benefits	Physical harm	Respect from superiors, peers, and customers	Growth
1. Good pay for my work—important.	.62	-.20	-.03	.08	.08
2. Good pay for my work—more.	.70	-.04	-.02	-.38	.14
3. Frequent raises in pay—important.	.74	-.13	-.27	-.01	.04
4. Frequent raises in pay—more.	.76	-.16	-.08	-.35	.04
5. Frequent improvements in fringe benefits—important.	-.28	.64	.37	-.11	-.06
6. Frequent improvements in fringe benefits—more.	-.13	.83	.06	.25	-.12
7. A complete fringe benefit program—important.	-.38	.23	.15	-.03	-.13
8. A complete fringe benefit program—more.	-.21	.75	.15	(.43)	-.15
9. Feeling safe from physical danger—important.	-.15	.07	.86	.07	-.05
10. Feeling safe from physical danger—more.	-.01	(.40)	.50	(.50)	-.07
11. A sense of security from bodily harm—important.	-.15	.08	.86	.02	.05
12. A sense of security from bodily harm—more.	-.09	.39	.47	(.51)	-.02
13. Respect from my boss—important.	-.04	.16	.08	-.13	-.13
14. Respect from my boss—more.	-.12	-.06	.06	.75	-.16
15. Openness and honesty between my boss and me—important.	.00	.03	.03	-.11	-.07
16. Openness and honesty between my boss and me—more.	-.10	-.05	.07	.84	-.05

17. Mutual trust between my boss and me—important.	-.13	.01	.04	-.08	-.08
18. Mutual trust between my boss and me—more.	-.10	.11	.00	.85	-.04
19. Cooperative relations with my coworkers—important.	-.03	-.08	.14	.14	.10
20. Cooperative relations with my coworkers—more.	-.02	.12	.08	.78	-.09
21. Respect from my coworkers—important.	.16	.15	.08	.16	-.18
22. Respect from my coworkers—more.	-.02	.17	.02	.80	.02
23. Openness and honesty with my coworkers—important.	-.14	.05	.15	.00	-.19
24. Openness and honesty with my coworkers—more.	-.02	.19	.00	.82	.00
25. Friendly, cordial relations with customers—important.	.06	-.12	.23	.03	-.10
26. Friendly, cordial relations with customers—more.	-.01	.22	.03	.73	-.03
27. Respect from customers—important.	-.02	.08	.14	.08	.04
28. Respect from customers—more.	-.17	.22	-.01	.73	-.08
29. Developing new skills and knowledge at work—important.	.16	-.06	-.06	.05	.46
30. Developing new skills and knowledge at work—more.	.03	-.08	-.12	-.22	.61
31. Being challenged by my work—important.	.07	.02	.07	.03	.75
32. Being challenged by my work—more.	.00	-.29	.06	(.45)	.66
33. Making full use of my abilities at work—important.	.02	-.09	-.06	-.07	.56
34. Making full use of my abilities at work—more.	.13	-.14	.06	(.49)	.47

* Note: Items underlined were expected to load on the specific factors while items in parentheses were not expected to have high loadings where they did.

above .40 on this factor. All six of the items which were expected to form a desire for growth factor had loadings above .45 on a single factor, and no other items had loadings above .19 on this factor. But two growth items had loadings above .40 on another factor.

The general picture which evolves from the E.R.G. item factor analysis is a replication of previous results plus an extension to the new variables. Yet the results were not all simple structure nor identical to the earlier findings. Like the earlier study, the peer satisfaction factor had lower internal consistency than the other satisfaction measures. Overall, the internal consistency of satisfaction items tended to be greater than for desire items, and the discrimination between factors for these items was greater as well. The fact that the relatedness desire scales loaded only on the "more" items was consistent with the earlier results (Alderfer, 1967). Most surprising was the failure of the replication study to find discrimination among the desire measures for various significant others. Instead, a general factor indicating a desire for more open and trusting relations with all three types of significant others emerged.

As a consequence of these findings, desire scales for existence and growth needs were formed by summing "importance" and "more" ratings, while desire scales for relatedness needs were formed by summing only "more" items.

E.R.G. Chronic Desire Scales The Recruitment Interviews study provided an opportunity to obtain split-half reliability measures for the chronic desire scales. Six E.R.G. chronic needs were listed in two lists of eleven job factors which the respondents were asked to rank and then distribute points. The first list of factors contained a different set of "filler" items, than the second list, and the E.R.G. items appeared in a different order on the two lists. Respondents were asked not to look back at their answers to the first list when they completed the second one.

Table 5-4 contains Spearman-Brown reliability estimates based on the correlations between rankings (converted to "T" scores) and between point assignments from the two lists. The range of coefficients was from .63 to .88. With one exception, the point scales gave higher reliabilities than the rankings.

Maslow Satisfaction Scales In the Bank study, Maslow satisfaction items were developed by making statements from Schneider's stems by adding "I do" in front of each stem. These items appeared in the agree-disagree format and were mixed among the E.R.G. items.

Table 5-4. Reliabilities for Chronic Desire Scales (n = 112)

	Ranking scales	*Point scales*
Pay	.73	.81
Fringe benefits	.80	.67
Respect from superiors	.86	.86
Respect from peers	.73	.84
Use of skills and abilities	.63	.83
Learning opportunities	.69	.88

Table 5-5 shows the results of factor analyzing the Maslow satisfaction items. Four of the seven items expected to form a security factor had loadings above .43 on a single factor, but this factor also had two social items with loadings above .43 and four esteem items with loadings above .40. There appeared to be two factors where social items predominated. The first social factor was defined primarily by two items which characterized people as friendly and cooperative. Both of these items had loadings above .70 and no other items had loadings on this factor above .32. The second social factor was defined primarily by three items with loadings above .46, all of which had interaction and contact with others as a predominant theme. No other items had loadings above .19 on this factor. Three of seven esteem items had loadings above .47 on the same factor, and no other items had loadings above .33 on this factor. Three of seven autonomy items had loadings above .48 on the same factor, and one social item also had a loading above .41 on this factor. All seven of the self-actualization items had loadings above .41 on the same factor. This factor also included two autonomy items with loadings above .60 and three esteem items with loadings above .40.

Maslow desire items for the Bank study were developed by taking Schneider's stems and using them in the "importance" and "more" formats. Table 5-6 shows the results of factor analyzing the Maslow desire items. Only the two factors accounting for the most variance from this analysis have been presented because the results do not lend themselves to a theoretical interpretation. The first factor had

Table 5-5. Maslow Satisfaction Items from Schneider Scales Factor Analysis (Format changed)

Item (stem for "I do things . . .")	Security	(1) Social	(2) Social	Esteem	Autonomy	Self actualiza- tion
Security						
1. that make me feel safe when I am doing them.	.64	.13	.16	-.21	.04	-.16
2. which make me feel relaxed.	.72	.14	.01	.08	-.02	-.01
3. which I am content to do.	.60	.07	-.03	-.10	.06	.28
4. that are easy for me,	.10	-.18	-.09	.33	.04	-.30
5. that are familiar.	.44	.02	.16	.14	.17	-.28
6. that look like they will benefit me in the future.	.22	.20	-.04	-.01	.05	.35
7. which make me feel comfortable.	.73	.23	.13	.15	.09	.03
Social						
8. with people who are cooperative.	.26	.72	.09	-.13	.17	-.12
9. with people who are friendly.	.28	.80	.00	.04	.04	.04
10. in which I have the opportunity to develop close friendships.	(.44)	-.06	.47	-.14	-.06	.30
11. which are helpful to others.	.12	.08	.00	.20	.12	.18
12. best when others are around.	-.01	-.05	.86	.10	-.06	.07
13. when others are around.	-.03	-.04	.54	.28	(.42)	-.22
14. where I am liked by others.	(.46)	.32	-.10	.19	-.05	.03
Esteem						
15. that make me feel intelligent.	(.50)	.06	.05	.10	.22	(.41)
16. where others tell me how smart I am.	.32	.03	-.09	.55	.10	.15

Item						
17. which give me a feeling of prestige.	(.41)	-.03	.17	.32	-.04	(.55)
18. that give me a feeling of self esteem.	(.44)	.04	.14	.19	.13	(.43)
19. that make me feel smart.	(.51)	.12	.19	.48	.15	.39
20. for which my accomplishments are recognized.	.03	.18	-.02	.20	-.22	.35
21. that I feel I do better than anyone else.	-.06	-.05	-.03	.78	.04	.09
Autonomy						
22. that I want to do.	.08	.21	.00	.05	.11	.20
23. where I can find solutions to problems on my own.	-.01	.26	.04	.16	.49	.18
24. where I can determine the way they are done.	.29	-.09	.01	-.07	.51	.28
25. where I can define the problem to be worked on.	.12	-.03	-.09	-.13	.17	.22
26. where I can be independent.	.13	-.08	.00	-.08	.72	.30
27. in which I have a lot of opportunity for independent thought and action.	-.09	.16	.06	-.02	.37	(.60)
28. where I have a lot of authority.	-.13	-.19	-.05	.17	.16	(.61)
Self-actualization						
29. where I can be creative.	-.08	-.26	-.09	.06	.07	.71
30. I am dedicated to.	.25	-.05	.16	-.06	.00	.42
31. where I can perform up to my abilities.	.25	.15	.02	-.13	.22	.63
32. which give me a feeling of worthwhile accomplishment.	.20	-.03	-.01	-.01	.18	.61
33. that give me a feeling of self-fulfillment.	.22	.13	-.01	.00	.18	.76
34. where I can be imaginative.	-.20	-.11	.06	.12	.12	.80
35. that allow me to realize my potentialities.	.15	-.08	-.04	.13	-.02	.70

Note: Items underlined were expected to load on the specific factors while items in parentheses were not expected to have high loadings where they did.

loadings greater than .40 on all the "more" items, regardless of which concept an item was based upon. The second factor had loadings of more than .64 on the "importance" items from the autonomy and self-actualization concepts.

Table 5-6. Maslow Desire Items Factor Analysis

	I	*II*
1. Having a sense of security—importance.	.12	.15
2. Having a sense of security—more.	.74	−.09
3. Being accepted by others—importance.	−.06	.25
4. Being accepted by others—more.	.69	−.04
5. The opportunity to develop close friendships at work—importance.	.17	.03
6. The opportunity to develop close friendships at work—more.	.68	.12
7. Being liked by others—importance.	.12	.18
8. Being liked by others—more.	.71	−.05
9. The feeling of prestige—importance.	.11	.19
10. The feeling of prestige—more.	.49	.00
11. A sense of self-esteem—importance.	.13	.48
12. A sense of self-esteem—more.	.75	.14
13. Opportunity for independent thought and action—importance.	.08	.72
14. Opportunity for independent thought and action—more.	.74	.18
15. Thinking for myself—importance.	.06	.71
16. Thinking for myself—more.	.79	.13
17. Feeling a sense of self-fulfillment—importance.	.00	.65
18. Feeling a sense of self-fulfillment—more.	.67	.17
19. Opportunities for personal growth and development—importance.	.14	.80
20. Opportunities for personal growth and development—more.	.66	.37

The results of factor analyzing the Maslow items indicate that there is considerably less convergence among items designed to measure the same concept and less discrimination among items intended to measure different concepts than there were for the E.R.G. items. As with the E.R.G. items, the convergence and discrimination is better for satisfaction items than for desire items.

These results raise a number of questions and suggest some tentative conclusions about the current operationality of the two theories. One set of questions concerns the degree to which there was evidence for the kind of overlap between need categories which was suggested in Chapter 2 (Figure 2-3). To test for this possibility, unit weights were given to those Maslow items which were expected to measure particular concepts, and these scales were correlated with the E.R.G. scales. Table 5-7 contains the results of this analysis.

Table 5-7. Correlations between Schneider Measures of Maslow Need Satisfaction and E.R.G. Measures of Need Satisfaction† (n = 217)

	Schneider scales				
E.R.G. Scales	*Security*	*Social*	*Esteem*	*Autonomy*	*Self-actualization*
Pay	.01	.04	.15*	.16*	.31*
Fringe benefits	.09	.14*	.13	.02	.08
Physical danger	.05	.13	.10	.13	.20*
Superiors	.15*	.18*	.19*	.22*	.33*
Peers	−.03	.22*	.10	.20*	.32*
Growth	−.03	.06	.34*	.45*	.68*

* $p < .02$

† □ indicates that part of the table where overlap between concepts would have predicted correlations among scales.

The relatively high correlation between self-actualization and growth was expected from the conceptual analysis. The correlations of autonomy and esteem with growth form a decreasing pattern according to their order in the hierarchy and therefore tend to support the kind of overlap among the higher-order Maslow categories which was proposed by the E.R.G. analysis. By observing the factor loadings among the Maslow items, one would also have expected the summed scales to correlate as they did; the self-actualization factor had substantial loadings from both esteem and autonomy items. There were significant correlations between the Maslow social scale and the E.R.G. peers and superiors scales, as expected. The significant correlation of the E.R.G. superiors scale with both the Maslow security and the esteem scales was also expected. The one place where significant correlations were expected and not found was between the Maslow security scale and the E.R.G. pay, fringe benefits, and physical danger scales. From these results it would appear the security scale as designed was slightly interpersonally oriented and not relevant to material concerns.[1]

From the results obtained in these studies it would appear that Maslow's theory is less operationally defined than the E.R.G. theory. The question of measurement precedes actual testing of the theories. It is not quite the same thing to find that one has not been able to make a theory operational as it is, to make it operational and then find its predictions disconfirmed. At the same time, not all parts of Maslow's theory remain undefined operationally. The self-actualization measures seem to show the highest convergence across satisfactions and desires and between the two models, thereby providing some empirical support for a conclusion which had been reached earlier from conceptual and empirical analyses.

One way that the Maslow measures differ from the E.R.G. scales is in specificity. E.R.G. items refer to more precise objects than the Maslow items do. Could this fact by itself lead to greater convergence among items which have the same target (e.g., pay, fringe benefits, superiors, etc.)? It is true that E.R.G. theory includes mechanisms whereby specific needs within each category can be defined while Maslow's theory does not. The existence of greater specificity, therefore, does not occur independently of theoretical considerations. But does the greater specificity by itself, on methodological grounds alone, account for the greater convergence and discrimination of the E.R.G. items? There can be little doubt that it contributes to the internal consistency of the scales, but there is also evidence that the other content of the items beyond their object also contributes because some items (such as no. 19 under superiors satisfaction), which have the same object, do not load very high or even in the same direction as other items sharing that object.

---

[1] There were other correlations in Table 5-7 which were not predicted from the conceptual analysis. They include the positive relations between self-actualization and pay, physical danger, superiors, and peers; between pay and esteem and autonomy; and between autonomy and peers and superiors. These findings are interesting in themselves and support the operation of other variables than those covered by need theory.

PREDICTIVE VALIDITY

Most of the field studies provided opportunities to obtain correlations between the E.R.G. satisfaction measures and other variables external to those included in the theory. The concept of satisfaction as it is proposed by the E.R.G. theory conceives of a person in contact with aspects of his external world. Need satisfaction (or frustration) comes to a person as he perceives the degree that he is able to engage in processes which enable him to reach the ends he seeks. Certain environmental conditions are more likely to allow various satisfactions to happen. These have been examined in the form of several organizational and demographic variables. Certain other attitudes and behaviors might also be expected to correlate with need satisfaction and these, too, were investigated.

Organizational and Demographic Variables

In each of the business organizations, the correlations between need satisfactions and organization variables have been presented separately for managerial and nonmanagerial personnel. Hypotheses based both on social class analyses and on organizational structure suggest that these two groups are sufficiently different that their separate analysis is warranted. One should bear in mind that some of the relationships to be observed are to some unknown degree affected by the unique qualities of the specific organizations, and, therefore, may not be general to all systems.

For the Manufacturing employees, the results shown in Table 5-8 indicate that pay satisfaction was positively correlated with job complexity, seniority, and annual pay. Satisfaction with one's supervisory relationship was negatively correlated with job complexity and education. Growth satisfaction was positively correlated with job complexity, seniority, and annual pay.

Among the Manufacturing managers, the results shown in Table 5-9 indicate that satisfaction with one's supervisory relationship was positively related to job level. Growth satisfaction was positively correlated with job complexity. Consequently for both groups in this organization, growth satisfaction was positively correlated with job complexity. At the same time, satisfaction with one's supervisory relationship was correlated to job complexity in opposite directions.

Annual pay was positively correlated to pay satisfaction for employees but not for managers.

Table 5-8. Correlations between Need Satisfactions and Organization Variables for Manufacturing Employees

(n = 138)

	Job complexity	Education	Seniority	Annual pay
Pay satisfaction	.21*	−.08	.28†	.28†
Fringe benefits satisfaction	.02	−.08	.03	−.05
Superior relationship satisfaction	−.17*	−.17*	−.13	−.14
Peer relationship satisfaction	−.03	.02	−.08	−.04
Growth satisfaction	.37†	−.10	.20*	.23†

* $p < .05$ † $p < .01$

Table 5-9. Correlations between Need Satisfactions and Organization Variables for Manufacturing Managers

(n = 34)

	Job complexity	Education	Seniority	Annual pay
Pay satisfaction	.24	−.13	.24	.04
Fringe benefits satisfaction	−.03	−.07	.21	.10
Superior relationship satisfaction	.32*	.24	.02	.25
Peer relationship satisfaction	.22	.15	−.01	.16
Growth satisfaction	.29*	−.07	.15	.22

* $p < .05$

For the Bank employees, the results shown in Table 5-10 indicate that pay satisfaction was negatively correlated with education. Fringe benefits satisfaction was negatively correlated with seniority and annual pay and positively correlated with being a woman. Physical-danger satisfaction was negatively correlated with having job duties involving customer contact. Satisfaction with one's relationship with peers was negatively correlated with being a woman. Satisfaction with customer relationships was positively related to job complexity. Growth satisfaction was positively related to job complexity, annual pay, and with being a man.

For the Bank officers, the results shown in Table 5-11 indicate that pay satisfaction was positively related to job complexity, seniority, and annual pay. Fringe benefits satisfaction was positively related to the same three organizational variables, although the pattern of sizes among the correlations differed. For pay satisfaction the highest correlation was with annual pay while for fringe benefits satisfaction, the highest correlation was with seniority. Physical danger satisfaction was positively related to education. Satisfaction with one's supervisory relationship was positively related to job complexity and customer-contact activities. Satisfaction with one's peer relationships was positively related to job complexity, customer-contact activities, education, and annual pay. Customer-relations satisfaction was positively related to job complexity, customer-contact activities, seniority, and annual pay. Growth satisfaction was positively related to job complexity, customer-contact activities, seniority, and annual pay.

The differences among the observed correlations is quite marked between the officers and employees. The correlation between pay satisfaction and education was significantly negative for employees and insignificantly positive for officers. Annual pay and seniority were both positively related to pay satisfaction for officers but showed no such associations among employees. Physical danger satisfaction was negatively related to customer contact for employees and insignificantly positively related to customer contact for officers. Satisfaction with one's supervisory relationship was not significantly related to any organization variables among employees, but it was positively related to job complexity and customer contact for officers. Peer relationship satisfaction was related only to sex among employees while it was positively related to job complexity, customer contact activity, seniority, and annual pay for officers. Customer relationship satisfaction was positively related to seniority and annual pay for officers but not for employees. Only growth satisfaction was positively related to essentially the same variables for both officers

Table 5-10. Correlations between E.R.G. Need Satisfactions and Organization Variables for Bank Employees

(n = 157)

	Job complexity	Customer contact activities	Education	Seniority	Annual pay	Sex (2 = F 1 = M)
Pay satisfaction	.06	-.02	-.16*	-.01	.02	-.07
Fringe benefits satisfaction	-.06	-.04	-.08	-.17*	-.19*	.24†
Physical danger satisfaction	-.07	-.24†	.10	.08	.11	-.07
Superiors relationship satisfaction	.04	-.11	-.14	-.09	.11	-.09
Peers relationship satisfaction	-.03	-.11	-.12	.00	.11	-.27†
Customers relationship satisfaction	.17*	.15	-.07	.08	.12	-.02
Growth satisfaction	.30†	.15	.08	.14	.32†	-.24†

* $p < .05$ † $p < .01$

Table 5-11. Correlations between E.R.G. Need Satisfactions and Organization Variables for Bank Officers

(n = 60)

	Job complexity	Customer contact activities	Education	Seniority	Annual pay
Pay satisfaction	.36†	.19	.13	.26†	.41†
Fringe benefits satisfaction	.32†	.18	-.01	.37†	.28†
Physical danger satisfaction	.18	.11	.26†	.06	.00
Superiors relationship satisfaction	.28†	.32†	-.09	.10	.20
Peers relationship satisfaction	.26†	.33†	.23*	-.17	.26†
Customers relationship satisfaction	.31†	.24†	-.06	.25†	.28†
Growth satisfaction	.28†	.30†	-.15	.21*	.24*

$*p < .05$ $†p < .01$

and employees. They were job complexity, customer-contact activity, and annual pay.

The results from Manufacturing and Bank show that the need satisfaction measures can detect relationships with organization variables that differ between hierarchical groupings within and between business organizations of quite different purposes. With organizations that are as different as a manufacturing firm and a bank, one has a comparison that tends to maximise the variance in organizational conditions. The two fraternities, on the other hand, were quite similar in purpose, size, and location.

In Alpha House, the results shown in Table 5-12 indicate that financial satisfaction was positively correlated with the number of house members seen on an average day, living in the house, and sociometric choice. It was also negatively correlated with grade-point average. Satisfaction with peer relationships was positively correlated with number of offices held, living in the house, and sociometric choice. Growth from house activities satisfaction was positively related to sociometric choice. For Beta House, results also shown in Table 5-12 indicate that peer relationships satisfaction was positively related to sociometric choice, and growth from house activities was negatively related to grade-point average.

Both houses showed a positive correlation between sociometric choice and peer relationships satisfaction. But the negative correlation between growth from house activities satisfaction was substantially stronger in Beta House than in Alpha House. Moreover, there was a positive relationship between peer relationships satisfaction and number of offices held in Alpha House but none in Beta House. There was a positive correlation between living in Alpha House and financial satisfaction but the same relationship was negative in Beta House. Sociometric choice was positively correlated with financial satisfaction in Alpha House but not in Beta House.

Many of the observed correlations in the four organizations could have been expected on *a priori* grounds. The general finding of a positive association between growth satisfaction and job complexity across both types of business organization and within both hourly and management groups was expected. Also predictable was the positive correlation between sociometric choice and peer relationship satisfaction which was found in both fraternities. We expected to

Table 5-12. Correlations between Need Satisfactions and Organization Variables for Fraternities

	Number of offices held	Number of members seen	Living (In = 2 Out = 1)	Grade point average	Sociometric choice
Alpha House (n = 57)					
Financial satisfaction	.16	.28†	.29†	-.21*	.34†
Peer relationships satisfaction	.34†	.16	.26*	.03	.38†
Growth satisfaction from house activities	.08	.18	.10	-.18	.22*
Growth satisfaction from academic activities	.00	.11	-.05	.05	-.11
Beta House (n = 46)					
Financial satisfaction	.14	.21	-.21	-.04	-.02
Peer relationships satisfaction	.01	.11	.08	.03	.28†
Growth satisfaction from house activities	-.08	.14	.11	-.38†	.21
Growth satisfaction from academic activities	.04	-.06	.00	.18	-.07

* $p < .05$ † $p < .01$

find a positive correlation between annual pay and pay satisfaction that held across employment status, but instead found it only for Manufacturing employees and Bank officers. We did expect to find physical danger satisfaction negatively correlated with customer-contact activities for employees but not for officers in the Bank study. It was not surprising to find fringe benefits satisfaction positively associated with seniority for Bank officers. In the fraternity studies, we did expect the number of offices held to be correlated with growth satisfaction from house activities but this was not found in either setting. We also expected growth satisfaction from academic activities to be correlated with grade-point average, but found this to be true in neither house. Many of the other correlations could not have been predicted in advance and perhaps reflect either unique characteristics of the particular systems or limitations in our current knowledge.

Nevertheless, these results do show evidence that the need satisfaction scales correlate in understandable ways with organization variables external to the E.R.G. theoretical system and thereby provide evidence for the measures' predictive validity.

Attitude and Behavior Variables

The Bank study also provided an opportunity to measure attitudes other than needs and therefore to analyze the relationships between need satisfaction and other work related attitudes. The results of these analyses are shown in Tables 5-13 and 5-14. Among Bank employees, job involvement was positively correlated with peer relationship satisfaction, customer relationship satisfaction, and growth satisfaction. Job satisfaction, organizational satisfaction, and confidence in top management were positively related to all of the need satisfaction measures except physical danger satisfaction. Confidence in one's superior was positively related to all of the need satisfaction measures. Tension and fatigue were negatively related to pay, physical danger, superior relationship, and peer relationship satisfactions.

For the Bank officers, involvement was related only to pay satisfaction. Job satisfaction was positively related to physical danger, superiors relationship, peer relationship, and growth satisfactions. Organization satisfaction was positively related to pay, fringe benefits, superiors relationship, peer relationship, and customer relationship satisfaction. Confidence in one's superior and confidence in top management were both related to pay, fringe benefits, superiors relationship, peers relationship, and customer relationship satisfaction. In addition, top management confidence was related to growth satisfaction while superior confidence was not. Tension was positively related to physical danger satisfaction and to growth satisfaction, while fatigue was negatively related to physical danger satisfaction and customer relationship satisfaction.

As with the relationships between need satisfactions and organizational variables, the employees and officers showed some markedly different correlations between need satisfactions and other job-related attitudes. For the employees, job involvement was most strongly related to several relatedness satisfactions and growth satisfaction, while for officers, it was only related to pay satisfaction. Job satisfaction was related to more kinds of need satisfaction for employees than for officers, while organization satisfaction was positively related to many need satisfactions for both groups. Confidence in one's own superior and in top management was positively related to many need satisfactions in both groups. Among the employees, tension and fatigue were *negatively* related to several existence and relatedness needs, while for officers, tension was *positively* related to growth satisfaction and physical danger satisfaction.

Several of these observed relationships had been predicted. Job and organization satisfaction were expected to correlate with most of the need satisfaction measures. Confidence in one's superior was expected to correlate very positively with superiors relationship and peers relationship satisfaction. We also expected tension to correlate negatively with existence and relatedness satisfactions and positively with growth satisfaction, but did not expect these predictions to split between officers and employees. We expected job involvement to correlate positively with growth satisfaction for both employee and officer groups, not just for employees as was found.

During the Adolescent Laboratory, behavior ratings on the dimensions of participation, expressing feelings, and trying new behavior were obtained by asking the participants to rate each other's behavior at the same time as they completed the need satisfaction scales. Table 5-15 contains the resulting correlations. Satisfaction

Table 5-13. Correlations between E.R.G. Need Satisfactions and Other Job Related Attitudes for Bank Employees

(n=157)

	Involvement	Job satisfaction	Organizational satisfaction	Top management confidence	Tension	Fatigue	Superior Confidence
Pay satisfaction	.04	.36†	.42†	.22†	-.23†	-.22†	.23†
Fringe benefits satisfaction	-.06	.23†	.35†	.30†	-.07	-.07	.25†
Physical danger satisfaction	.12	.09	.08	.11	-.19*	-.21†	.22†
Superiors relationship satisfaction	.09	.52†	.47†	.56†	.24†	-.29†	.73†
Peers relationship satisfaction	.23†	.34†	.41†	.30†	.16*	-.23†	.50†
Customers relationship satisfaction	.24†	.25†	.35†	.25†	-.07	-.07	.29†
Growth satisfaction	.44†	.57†	.38†	.30†	.05	-.05	.30†

* $p < .05$ † $p < .01$

Table 5-14. Correlations between E.R.G. Need Satisfaction and Other Job Related Attitudes for Bank Officers

(n=60)

	Involvement	Job satisfaction	Organizational satisfaction	Top management confidence	Tension	Fatigue	Superior confidence
Pay satisfaction	.22*	.00	.49†	.45†	-.11	-.06	.54†
Fringe benefits satisfaction	.08	-.05	.36†	.43†	.04	-.15	.41†
Physical danger satisfaction	-.16	.22*	.03	.00	.22†	-.21*	.10
Superiors relationship satisfaction	.06	.22*	.37†	.34†	-.08	.05	.48†
Peers relationship satisfaction	-.04	.22*	.44†	.34†	-.10	.04	.24*
Customers relationship satisfaction	.13	.11	.45†	.31†	-.05	-.25†	.48†
Growth satisfaction	.11	.44†	.16	.32†	.27†	-.13	.07

* $p < .05$ † $p < .01$

with staff relationships was positively correlated with participation and expressing feelings. Satisfaction with group relationships was positively related to participation, expressing feelings, and trying new behavior. Growth satisfaction was positively related to expressing feelings and trying new behavior. All of these correlations were expected.

Table 5-15. **Correlations between Need Satisfaction and Observed Behaviors in Adolescent Lab**

(n = 83)

	Participation	Expressing feelings	Trying new behavior
Satisfaction with staff relationships	.22*	.30†	.17
Satisfaction with group relationships	.32†	.37†	.41†
Satisfaction with growth	.14	.22*	.29†

* $p < .05$ † $p < .01$

Summary and Conclusions The purpose of this chapter was to address the empirical validity of the E.R.G. measures and where possible do the same for measures of Maslow's concepts. For the most part, E.R.G. measures showed substantial convergent and discriminant validity. Satisfaction measures showed greater discrimination among specific needs than desire scales. Relatedness need scales showed the greatest uncertainty whether the variable was a satisfaction or a desire and whether the concept was from the E.R.G. theory or from Maslow's theory. Except for the self-actualization concept, items based on Maslow's concepts showed relatively little convergence or discrimination in ways that one would expect from the theory. Like the E.R.G. scales, attempts to obtain convergence from Maslow desire scales showed less success than convergence among satisfaction scales. Generally speaking, E.R.G. measures fared better than the Maslow measures, except for the self-actualization concept whose measurement properties were about the same as the growth concept's.

Almost all of the E.R.G. satisfaction measures showed one or more correlations with organization variables, attitudes, or behavior. As a consequence, we may conclude from these results that the scales in general have convergent, discriminant, and predictive validity, although there were a few exceptions to this statement. In the subsequent chapters we shall report the support received by predictions from E.R.G. theory in the various organizational settings.

Chapter 6

EXISTENCE DESIRES

Existence needs are the most concrete and least ambiguous of human desires. Lack of some satisfaction of these needs can threaten the material survival of an organism. For these reasons, they may be termed the most basic of human needs. Some represent the various physiological needs of man and may have somatic sources in the human body. All are potentially scarce and therefore can generate situations where one person's gain becomes another person's loss.

When there is no shortage of food or water, each person desiring these substances can obtain what he wants. However, let there be a limited supply of either substance and one person's satisfaction becomes correlated with another person's frustration. Physical rest may be a need which is not so obvious in fitting this formula. Each person has the capacity for rest. The scarce resource is not human capacity but *time* free from other activities. What about protection from physical danger? The means of protection require the use of material substances, perhaps weapons or shields. In both cases, the gain of one party under conditions of scarcity is directly correlated with the loss of another party.

Nonphysiological existence needs share the same property. One might consider the "classic" demands of labor for wages, hours, benefits, and conditions. As long as these are the ends for which management and labor seek, there can be no doubt that one party's gain is correlated with the other's loss. Perhaps a less obvious example is physical working conditions. Again one must be careful in thinking about what resource it is that is being sought. For physical working conditions the resource is space of a certain quality. When space is limited, giving better conditions (for example, in the form of air conditioning, lighting, decorations, or facilities) to one party is directly correlated with giving poorer conditions to another party and, therefore, with satisfying one party at the expense of dissatisfying another.

It is this property of creating realistic (and therefore also fantasized) win-lose (or zero-sum game) situations that provides the hypothetical unifying feature among those various material ends termed existence needs. The term existence is used because if a party (be it person, group, organization, or community) is sufficiently frustrated in its attempts to obtain adequate material resources, then the physical existence of that party is severely threatened. Since very few material substances are limitless in supply, almost any human unit at some time faces some degree of threat to its physical existence.

E.R.G. theory contains two propositions concerning factors which tend to increase the strength of existence desires. As with the entire theory, these propositions are intended to be dynamic in that they propose correlations among changes through time. However, the data that will be presented in this chapter represent only tests of static derivations from the model.

The first proposition predicting to variations in the strength of existence desires is:

P1. The less existence needs are satisfied, the more they will be desired.

Two aspects of this proposition are especially worthy of attention because they may not be immediately obvious from reading the statement. First, the proposition subsumes what earlier has been termed "the simple frustration hypothesis" and specifies its application to existence needs. Applied to existence needs, this simply says that a person wants that particular material substance which he feels he is not adequately receiving. While it accounts for the simple frustration hypothesis in the realm of existence needs, the proposition is also more general than just that. It also says that lacking satisfaction with regard to one material end, a person will seek other material ends as substitutes. Thus, not only will a man who feels deprived in the area of pay seek more pay according to this proposition, but he will also seek more fringe benefits and more protection from physical danger.

The data presented in Table 6-1 present the results of one series of tests of proposition 1 utilizing static correlations computed from data obtained in several different organizational settings. In the two business organizations, separate analyses were made for the employee and managerial groups. These correlations were computed between satisfaction measures consisting of Likert scales of several items and five point rating scales of "more" and "importance" for desires. Typically, there were several items in each scale. The negative signs of the correlations in the table indicate that satisfaction was inversely related to desire.

The results shown in Table 6-1 provide rather strong support for proposition 1. Without exception in each group the satisfaction of a need was more strongly correlated with the desire for that particular need than for any "substitute" need. The range of correlations for the satisfaction and desires of needs themselves was from $-.76$ in Beta House to $-.25$ for Manufacturing employees.

The data from the fraternities differed from that obtained in the other settings because few brothers actually made money from being in a house. Rather, they were asked by the fraternity to pay dues for living, eating, and social expenses. The demand for material ends is really from the organization to the member rather than vice versa, as it is in Manufacturing and Bank. Consequently, the fraternity members were asked in their satisfaction measure whether they thought the financial demands were too great and in their desire measure to what degree they thought the financial demands on members should be reduced. In the other settings, the members were always asked how they felt about what they were getting materially and how much more they wanted.

The highest correlation found in Beta House may suggest that the potency of existence needs are higher as avoidance motives than as approach desires. That is, a person may tend to strive harder to avoid being placed in a situation where he has a limited supply of some material good than he would strive to be sure that he has more than he needs. Such a point would be consistent with the economists' view that there is a decreasing marginal utility for money.

In addition to the strong support shown for the "simple frustration hypothesis" aspect of proposition 1, there was also support shown for the "substitution" aspect of proposition 1. However, these correlations were not as high as the ones for the need itself, and in several cases they did not reach statistical significance. The three specific existence needs which were employed in these studies were pay, fringe benefits, and physical danger. One could readily argue that any observed relationship between pay satisfaction and benefits desire or between benefits satisfaction and pay desire exists primarily because both of these needs exist in a financial modality. However, the introduction of physical danger as a specific existence need results in a test of the hypothesis which is more general than using only dollar-oriented existence needs.

In the Bank study, satisfaction with physical safety showed significant negative correlations with desires for fringe benefits and satisfaction with fringe benefits was negatively related to desires for physical safety in the managerial group. But there were no significant relationships across the specific categories among the Bank employees.

Support for a relationship between benefits satisfaction and desire for physical safety was not an obvious finding, although it did follow from the theory. There is probably a reasonably widely held norm that a person can demand more in the way of pay and benefits for "hazardous duty." However, it is probably not as clear that a person feeling poorly covered by benefits should ask for more in terms of protection from physical harm.

Another aspect of the findings to be noted is that the observed correlations were generally higher in the managerial samples than among the employees. From the data reported in Chapter 5, one might have expected differences between organizations, rather than between groups on the existence dimensions. In Manufacturing, pay satisfaction was related to actual pay for employees but not for managers, while just the opposite was true in Bank. Perhaps the observed differences in the sizes of correlations reflect differences in actual reward structures faced by the groups. If the managers participate in a profit-sharing plan based on salary, then the link between pay and fringe benefits is more closely connected for them than for employees. Managers also may be more willing to speak for what they want through the vehicle of a research questionnaire as well. Neither of these possibilities was testable from the data collected.

A pattern can be discerned in the sizes of the relationship between satisfaction and desires among the various existence needs. Satisfaction and desire tend to be most highly negatively related for the need itself. Second highest among the correlations tend to be those involving substituting one need for another while remaining in the same modality, in this case financial. The least strong relationships tend to be between satisfaction of a need in one modality (e.g., financial) and desire in another modality (e.g., bodily harm). These additional qualifications show ways in which the general form of proposition 1 might be enriched and elaborated. The specific hypotheses deriving from proposition 1 which were tested in these studies represent only a subset of the possible hypotheses. Future research might profitably be directed toward the impact of frustrating more of the human physiological needs such as hunger and thirst.

Careful examination of the interconnections among the propositions of E.R.G. theory shows that there are two routes which would lead the satisfaction of one existence need to be related inversely to the desire for another. One mechanism is through the direct operation of proposition 1, and another is through the joint operation of propositions 1 and 8. While the first one prompted the hypotheses tested above, the second one may have contributed to some or all of the findings. The logic of the second (more indirect) route would be: (1) Frustration of e_1 leads to desire for e_1 (by $P1$) which, (2) leads to frustration of e_2 (by $P8$) which (3) leads to desire for e_2 (by $P1$). Without longitudinal data, it would not be possible to test for these separate effects.

In subsequent chapters, we shall have reason to consider the possibility of curvilinear relationships between satisfaction and desire for relatedness and growth needs. With this possibility in mind, we shall present a similar analysis for pay satisfaction and desire as the existence need for which the current data offers the widest variance in terms of actual pay. Among the respondents in these studies, the annual pay ranged from less than $4,000 to more than $40,000. To carry out this analysis, the Bank and Manufacturing samples were split into six nearly equal groups according to pay satisfaction, and then the desire mean for each satisfaction group was computed.

Table 6-1. Correlations for Hypotheses based on Proposition 1

(The less existence needs are satisfied, the more they will be desired.)

DESIRES

SATISFACTIONS	Managers			Employees		
	Pay	Fringe benefits	Physical safety	Pay	Fringe benefits	Physical safety
Manufacturing (n = 34, 138)						
Pay	-.61†	-.38†		-.30†	-.07	
Fringe benefits	-.37†	-.56†		-.21†	-.25†	
Bank (n = 60, 157)						
Pay	-.62†	-.48†	-.19	-.41†	-.13	.00
Fringe benefits	-.46†	-.59†	-.26*	-.11	-.48†	-.12
Physical safety	-.05	-.20*	-.33†	-.15	-.08	-.40†
Alpha House (n = 57)						
Financial demands	-.52†					
Beta House (n = 46)						
Financial demands	-.76†					

* p < .05   † p < .01

These data are shown in Table 6-2 where it can be seen that for each successive satisfaction group, desire decreases monotonically. There was no evidence for a curvilinear relationship between pay satisfaction and desire in either set of data.

Table 6-2. Pay Desire Means for Different Levels of Pay Satisfaction

	MANUFACTURING			BANK	
n	*Pay satisfaction*	*Pay desire*	*n*	*Pay satisfaction*	*Pay desire*
29	8.97	5.90	40	5.10	6.97
29	12.62	4.78	39	10.17	6.36
29	22.24	4.72	37	13.60	4.52
29	26.93	3.93	28	16.95	4.48
24	29.96	3.84	39	20.14	4.23
35	32.97	2.60	34	24.59	3.01

The second proposition predicting the variations of the strength of existence desires is:

P2. *The less relatedness needs are satisfied, the more existence needs will be desired.*

This proposition follows from the frustration-regression mechanism in E.R.G. theory. Existence goals are more concrete than relatedness goals. There is an old saying that one cannot purchase love or respect, but this proposition implies that under some circumstances a human being may try to obtain material ends as a substitute for valid and open interpersonal relationships. Perhaps there are two major ways that one might obtain substitute interpersonal gratification through making material demands. First, the art of making the demands serves at a minimum to maintain some contact in the relationship, no matter how interpersonally frustrating that contact might be. Perhaps some contact is better than none at all, even if the interaction produced by the contact has win-lose qualities and tends to foster a relationship in which the participants deal with each other more as material objects than as human beings. Second, a person may think he can replace the interpersonal esteem he feels from a satisfying relationship by various material indicators of esteem. It is usually easier to confront another person with requests for material things than with the fact that one's relationship is not working well, because the material request is more concrete. A person doing this exposes himself, reduces the likelihood of his exchange becoming emotional, and expresses some hostility at the same time. During one interview, a manager made the connection between his relatedness frustration and existence desires quite explicit. He had been asked the question of what important changes had taken place while he had been with the organization. He said many things in response to the question including:

My relationship with Mr. X (his boss) has been strictly a subordinate-superior relationship. He talks and I listen. This is about what it comes down to . . . I just do not feel . . . a sense of confidence with the man . . . I'm quite salary conscious and seem to be becoming increasingly so. If I were obtaining more nonfinancial satisfaction out of the job and I think one of the primary ones being that I were able to establish a rapport, this would be worth a lot of dollars . . . It would make less significant the dollar consideration. Since I don't have this, dollars loom even larger and therefore more important than they should.

Table 6-3 shows the results of testing hypotheses derived from proposition 2. Of the twenty-eight possible correlations in the table, all but three were in the predicted direction and nine were significant at the .05 level or less. Proposition 2 received support that was not as strong as that received by proposition 1. The step from human relationships to material needs is similar to the one among different material needs. In Table 6-1, six out of sixteen correlations relating one satisfaction to a different desire were significant at less than the .05 level.

The pattern of differential support for the hypotheses derived from proposition 2 provides some intriguing leads for establishing additional conditions under which proposition 2 might apply. Comparable instruments were administered in the fraternities, and comparison of mean differences between the houses indicated that both financial and relatedness satisfaction was higher in Alpha House than in Beta House (Alderfer and Lodahl, 1970). Manufacturing had a policy of paying both its employees and managers *above average rates* for comparable jobs, while Bank prided itself on meeting the average rates for similar jobs in other systems. We have already commented that Manufacturing had greater commitment to developing an organization that met member needs as well as organization goals than Bank did. Informal observations by the writer strongly suggested that Manufacturing members were more competent in dealing with human concerns than Bank members. These various bits of evidence tend to converge toward indicating that proposition 2 is more likely to apply where the absolute level of both existence and relatedness satisfactions is relatively low.

The fact that a range of specific existence and relatedness needs from different organizations and groups within organizations provide some measure of support for the proposition favors its generality. The range of support indicates that there is probably more to the observed relationships than a simple instrumentality such as a boss controlling his subordinates' pay, thereby making a good relationship with one's boss instrumental to getting paid well. A strictly instrumental argument would be strongest if the only place where the proposition received support was for the relationship between satisfaction with one's supervisory relationship and desire for pay in the business organizations.

Summary and Conclusions The results reported in this chapter showed support for both propositions 1 and 2 of the E.R.G. theory. The support was stronger for proposition 1 than for proposition 2. For proposition 1, it was possible to suggest ways to differentiate predictions of the strength of the relationships between the satisfaction of one specific need and the desire for another specific need. For proposition 2, it was possible to suggest conditions when it would most likely be valid. All of the support must be qualified by the fact that the data in this chapter were correlational (or cross-sectional) and thus did not test either the dynamic nature of the model or the direction of causality implied by the propositions.

However, with these qualifications in mind, one can identify the implications which these results have for the points of difference which E.R.G. theory has with Maslow's theory and the simple-frustration hypothesis. Support for proposition 1 could be seen as support for Maslow's theory as well as for E.R.G. theory. To take this view, one would necessarily be sloughing off some differences including Maslow's unwillingness to call pay a lower-level need (Maslow, 1965) and the ambiguity surrounding the definition of physiological and safety needs. Nevertheless, the basic thrust of proposition 1 is in the general spirit of Maslow's theory.

Table 6-3. Correlations for Hypotheses based on Proposition 2

(The less relatedness needs are satisfied, the more existence needs will be desired.)

DESIRES

RELATIONSHIP SATISFACTIONS	Managers			Employees		
	Pay	*Fringe benefits*	*Physical danger*	*Pay*	*Fringe benefits*	*Physical danger*
Manufacturing (*n*=34, 138)						
Superiors	-.21	-.33*		-.13	-.03	
Peers	-.10	-.16		-.05	-.20†	
Bank (*n*=60, 157)						
Superiors	-.35†	-.11	-.15	-.16*	-.08	.01
Peers	-.22*	-.19	-.26*	-.14*	.07	-.01
Customers	-.27*	-.23*	-.09	-.09	.05	-.01
Alpha House (*n*=57)						
Peers	-.19					
Beta House (*n*=46)						
Peers	-.27*					

* $p < .05$ † $p < .01$

Moreover, the overall support given to proposition 1 does call into question the adequacy of the simple frustration hypothesis. The observed relationships between the satisfaction of one specific need and the desire for another need would not be predicted by the simple-frustration hypothesis. However, proposition 1 subsumes the simple frustration hypothesis and makes these other predictions as well. Thus, it would appear that proposition 1 is more tenable than the simple frustration hypothesis.

Proposition 2 is a point where E.R.G. theory differs from Maslow's theory. Data supporting this proposition also support the E.R.G. approach over Maslow's views. Proposition 2 also would not be covered by the simple-frustration hypothesis and so data supporting it would also increase the relative merit of the E.R.G. theory in this comparison.

Chapter 7

RELATEDNESS DESIRES

Peoples require relationships with others in order to be fully human. The nature of human relationships is often difficult to determine, but it is possible for persons to develop a shared consensus about social reality by exposing and discussing their relevant emotions and perceptions. Years of research on human relationships, much of it growing out of a clinical or therapeutic tradition, have aided our understanding of how persons may frustrate their own attempts to develop satisfying relationships with each other. More recently a number of social inventions, such as the human relations training group, have provided additional clues about how people might go about developing more satisfying relationships with each other.

The concept of relatedness needs which is proposed by the E.R.G. theory owes much to writings of investigators such as Argyris (1962), Rogers (1959), Sullivan (1953), Storr (1961), Fromm (1956), and Horney (1937). In their work these writers have focussed on both the nature of interpersonal transactions which occur between people and on who the people are. Rogers, for example, has proposed that empathy, unconditional positive regard, and congruence are the necessary conditions for therapeutic personality change. Argyris (1962) has stated that relationships become more authentic as people are able to express themselves in ways that also permit others to be self-expressive. Fromm (1956) identified a number of different kinds of human love depending on the person with whom one exchanges emotions and on the nature (or limitations) of the emotions which are shared.

According to the E.R.G. theory, satisfying human relationships are achieved by persons who are psychologically significant to each other and who are able to share their relevant feelings and thoughts mutually. This means that both parties give and receive. Our assumption (backed by the research evidence in Chapter 3) is that the satisfaction of the parties in a relationship is positively correlated.

One is better at receiving the thoughts and feelings of another when he is able to give his own. One is able to give his own views better when he has been received accurately by another. Relatedness needs cannot be satisfied by win-lose outcomes, no matter which party wins or loses.

Significant others refers both to individuals of importance and to key human groupings. A parent, boss, sibling, or coworker would be a significant other, as would a family, a work group, an athletic team, or a voluntary organization. The concept of relatedness needs is intended to apply to an individual's relationship to the human units of various sizes from one person upward. A significant other is defined in terms of a known boundary defining the outside of a unit from the inside. In the case of a person, this boundary may be his skin, in the case of a group it might be the membership list.

Some approaches to human relationships either state directly or imply that satisfying relationships are characterized by the exchange of primarily, or only, positive emotions. The concept of satisfying relationships employed here emphasizes the exchange of all relevant emotions. It is difficult to imagine a lasting relationship where other than positive emotions did not become relevant. Respect, if it is used in a way that is consistent with its root (*respicere* = to look at), is a word that may be used to characterize the state of satisfying interpersonal relationships. A person who is respected by another is seen as he is in all of his unique individuality (Fromm, 1956).

In this chapter we shall deal with three major topics on the subject of interpersonal needs: (1) Testing hypotheses from the E.R.G. theory which predict how relatedness desires change as a function of various need satisfactions, (2) examining the relationships between satisfaction and desire for measures of Maslow's interpersonal needs, and (3) testing hypotheses from the E.R.G. propositions which predict how chronic relatedness needs affect relatedness satisfaction under different degrees of satisfaction.

E.R.G. HYPOTHESES

The first proposition predicting to variations in the strength of relatedness desires is:

*P*3. *The more existence needs are satisfied, the more relatedness needs will be desired.*

When people have been relieved of struggling for material ends by win-lose processes, then they may be more free to turn their attention to the development of satisfying human relationships. When the threat of material deprivation is reduced, then there may be less reason to view human relationships in win-lose terms. Maslow's theory is similar in spirit to proposition 3 although the reasoning is different. According to Maslow's view, higher order needs are less prepotent than physiological or safety needs. Thus, the interpersonal needs would tend not to emerge until some minimal level of satisfaction had been obtained for lower-order needs. Since the E.R.G. theory does not utilize the notion of prepotency of needs, this argument would not be part of the reasoning behind proposition 3. However, the general thrust of the proposition is essentially the same for both theories.

Table 7-1 presents the results of testing hypotheses based on proposition 3 in the various organizational settings. These results show no support at all for the proposition. Nine out of twenty-eight correlations (using a two-tailed test) were significant in the opposite direction. All but two of the correlations had signs in the opposite direction from that which was predicted.

These results were somewhat surprising in light of the support for the proposition found in other research. Even if one were to discard proposition 3 based on the data collected in the present studies, he would still be faced with the discrepancy between these results and the findings from other studies. How might this discrepancy be resolved? In none of the present studies were a substantial proportion of the respondents severely deprived materially. Many were quite affluent. Perhaps there was not enough variance in the negative portion of the scale for a test of proposition 3 to be made. Noting that the other research supporting the proposition came from hunger (food deprivation), a more bodily based need than pay or fringe benefits, one might also question whether the proposition might apply only to specific existence needs like hunger.

Neither of these possibilities, however, would account for the reversal of signs which was observed so markedly among the Bank employees. Of all the settings studied, this was probably the one which contained the most people who were genuinely deprived in a material sense. Perhaps these people "learned" that other persons, such as superiors, peers, and customers, could be instrumental to their material gain. They would want better relationships in order to achieve material gratification through them. This order of explanation goes beyond the scope of E.R.G. theory to involve learning mechanisms. It indicates some of the potential utility of developing ways of letting need theory and learning theory complement each other.

The second proposition predicting variations in the strength of relatedness desires is:

> *P*4. *The less relatedness needs are satisfied, the more they will be desired.*

This proposition contains a number of elements implicitly which should be made explicit. First, it subsumes the simple frustration hypothesis for relatedness needs in the same way that proposition 1 does for existence needs. Second, given the fact that specific relatedness needs are defined in terms of significant others, it proposes that the phenomenon of transference which has been readily observed in clinical settings is also more generally operative. While there is controversy among clinical theorists about how, if at all, the transference phenomena might be used for therapeutic gain, there is less disagreement about the existence of the phenomenon. Patients from time to time attempt to form relationships with the therapist that mirror unsatisfactory historical relationships. Motivating these efforts is a desire on the part of the patient to have the therapist substitute for some other significant figure in his life. Therapists, too, are prone to behave in similar ways, and their training is designed to reduce the likelihood of "countertransference." While transference has received rather extensive coverage in the clinical literature, it has been given only slight attention in the organizational literature (Zaleznik, 1966).

Table 7-1. Correlations for Hypotheses based on Proposition 3

(The more existence needs are satisfied, the more relatedness needs will be desired.)

| | DESIRES | | | | | |
| | Managers | | | Employees | | |
SATISFACTIONS	Superiors	Peers	Customers	Superiors	Peers	Customers
Manufacturing (n=34, 138)						
Pay	-.31	.01		-.16	.02	-.08
Fringe benefits	-.54	-.23		-.15	-.07	-.20
Bank (n=60, 157)						
Pay	-.09	-.14	-.15	-.18	-.17	-.23
Fringe benefits	-.11	-.13	-.10	-.19	-.18	
Physical safety	-.17	-.24	-.22	-.24	-.29	
Alpha House (n=57)						
Financial demands		-.20				
Beta House (n=46)						
Financial demands		-.01				

— significant in opposite direction at .05 or less

Table 7-2 shows static correlations testing hypotheses derived from proposition 4, and Table 7-3 shows the results of dynamic tests of hypotheses from proposition 4.

The results shown in Table 7-2 provide quite clearcut support for proposition 4. Generally speaking, satisfaction of a specific relatedness need was inversely correlated with desires for that and other relatedness needs. Most often satisfaction of a given relatedness need had the highest correlation with desire for that need itself. But there were exceptions to this generalization. Among the Manufacturing managers, satisfaction with their peer relationships was more negatively correlated with desires about the supervisor than with desires about peers. Among the Bank managers, satisfaction with customer relationships was (very slightly) more negatively related to desires about both superiors and peers than to desires about customers. These differential findings suggest that proposition 4 may be elaborated further in accordance with whether the person being satisfied is in a leadership position and whether the significant others with whom satisfaction is being sought are members of a defined group. For leaders, persons outside the group may be as significant or more significant than members inside the group. For group members other than the leader, persons outside the group may be less significant than members inside the group.

Alpha House, which had more satisfying interpersonal relationships overall than Beta House, showed a lower correlation between peer satisfaction and desire than Beta House (Alderfer and Lodahl, 1970). This finding suggests that the nature of the relationship between satisfaction and desire for relatedness needs may also depend on the absolute level of relatedness satisfaction. Data from human relations training laboratories become especially interesting in this connection because the quality of human interaction in these settings has been reported as more open and trusting than that found in more traditional organization settings (Argyris, 1969).

The results shown in Table 7-3 contain dynamic correlations for testing hypotheses derived from proposition 4. At Adult Lab, measurements of satisfaction and desire were taken at three points in time during the laboratory at about three-day intervals. At Boys School, two sets of measurements were taken, one before school opened in September and one $2\frac{1}{2}$ months later in the middle of

Table 7-2. Static Correlations for Hypotheses based on Proposition 4

(The less relatedness needs are satisfied, the more they will be desired.)

| | DESIRES | | | | | |
| | Managers | | | Employees | | |
RELATIONSHIP SATISFACTIONS	Superiors	Peers	Customers	Superiors	Peers	Customers
Manufacturing (n=34, 138)						
Superiors	-.70†	-.13		-.55†	-.20†	
Peers	-.44†	-.28*		-.34†	-.46†	
Bank (n=60, 157)						
Superiors	-.32†	-.19	-.15	-.44†	-.34†	-.19†
Peers	-.30*	-.36†	-.23*	-.34†	-.41†	-.17*
Customers	-.25*	-.24*	-.22*	-.18*	-.19†	-.17*
Alpha House (n=57)						
Peers		-.16				
Beta House (n=46)						
Peers		-.39†				

* p<.05   † p<.01

November. During the week in which Adult Lab took place, each successive measurement showed an increase in relatedness satisfaction. The means of staff satisfaction from t_1 to t_3 were 1.74, 4.82, and 9.89, while the means of group satisfaction for the same period were 3.20, 7.30, and 9.00. At Boys School, mean relatedness satisfaction decreased from 3.12 to 2.88 during the $2\frac{1}{2}$ months. Each dynamic correlation between the change in satisfaction and change in desires was paired with a corrected dynamic correlation. It is well known that change scores have a tendency to regress toward the mean and consequently that any change score tends to be negatively correlated with the initial value of the difference. Vroom (1966) proposed adjusting the correlations between changes for the initial values of both variables by partial correlation when it was known that there was no mean shift in either of the variables. In the present study, we knew that the satisfaction scores underwent mean changes while the desire scores did not. Consequently, adjusted correlations were computed by correlating the changes in satisfaction and desire while partialling out the initial value of the desire score. It can be seen that only one relationship became insignificant when this procedure was employed, although several were reduced in size.

The results show primarily positive correlations between changes in satisfaction and changes in desire for Adult Lab and a negative correlation from Boys School. Within Adult Lab, the correlations are more positive during the last half of the lab than during the first half. During the first part of the lab only changes in desires about the staff were significantly correlated with changes in relatedness satisfaction. During the latter portion of the lab, changes in both staff and group satisfaction were positively correlated with changes in both staff and group desires.

The dynamic correlations support the notion that the relationship between satisfaction and desire among relatedness needs depends on the absolute level of satisfaction. In Boys School, a traditional organization with many interpersonal problems (cf. Alderfer and Brown, 1970), the dynamic correlation between satisfaction and desire was negative. In Adult Lab, where new interpersonal behaviors were employed, the dynamic correlations between satisfaction and desire were positive and increased in size as time passed and relatedness satisfaction increased.

Table 7-3. Dynamic Correlations Relevant to Proposition 4

RELATIONSHIP SATISFACTIONS	DESIRES	
	Staff	Group
Adult Lab ($n=46$)		
t_1, t_2		
Staff	.34†	.17
	(.34)†	(.00)
Group	.30*	.09
	(.30)*	(−.03)
t_2, t_3		
Staff	.60†	.55†
	(.62)†	(.51)†
Group	.40†	.46†
	(.29)*	(.40)†
Boys School		Peers
Peers		−.19*
t_1, t_2		(−.12)

* $p<.05$ $p<.01$

Since the positive correlations appeared only in the human relations laboratory, one might wonder whether there might not be something about that type of setting which prompted the findings, other than its capacity to enable very satisfying interpersonal relationships to occur. In short, would the relationship between relatedness satisfaction and desire be positive in any place except a human relations laboratory? To answer this question the static data from Manufacturing, Bank, and the fraternities were reanalyzed by forming (as close as possible) equal groups of 25 to 34 respondents according to satisfaction level. The mean desire score for each group was computed. Table 7-4 presents these results.

The Bank data indicates that relatedness desires monotonically decrease as satisfaction increases for both superior and peer relationships. A similar pattern can be observed for peer relationships in Manufacturing. But for superior relationships in Manufacturing and for peer relationships in the fraternities, the association between satisfaction and desire was not monotonically decreasing at all points. In these cases, the most satisfied group showed an increase in desire in comparison to the second most satisfied group. Except for the most satisfied group, however, the relationship between satisfaction and desire was monotonically decreasing.[1] Thus static data from two traditional organizations indicated that a positive association between relatedness satisfaction and desire was not restricted to human relations laboratories. Moreover, the positive relationships were observed where one would expect them. We have noted before that Manufacturing had managers who were especially committed and trained to develop a humane organization, and the objectives of the fraternities were to establish meaningful and satisfying relations among the brothers.

Table 7-4. Relatedness Desire Means for Different Levels of Relatedness Satisfaction

MANUFACTURING

n	Superiors satisfaction	Superiors desire	n	Peers satisfaction	Superiors desire
31	3.90	6.22	30	7.90	4.13
26	12.15	4.58	30	15.83	2.73
21	16.80	3.57	25	18.84	2.32
26	20.11	1.80	32	22.12	1.91
38	22.47	1.21	35	25.03	1.68
34	25.73	1.32	24	28.67	1.25

BANK / COMBINED FRATERNITIES

n	Superiors satisfaction	Superiors desire	n	Peers satisfaction	Peers desire	n	Peers satisfaction	Peers desire
33	1.64	7.12	37	1.97	9.47	26	1.95	6.25
37	8.23	3.90	30	5.58	8.08	30	6.07	5.23
38	12.72	2.92	39	7.52	7.49	29	8.42	4.97
40	16.28	2.80	47	9.53	6.57	18	10.88	5.22
36	18.75	2.30	32	11.00	6.36			
33	22.91	1.92	32	13.33	6.18			

[1] The only place where the satisfaction and desire scales are comparable between organizations is with the fraternities and these data have been combined in order to provide larger samples. Consequently, direct comparison of satisfaction and desire scores between organizations was not possible.

The third proposition predicting to variations in the strength of relatedness desires is:

> *P5. The less growth needs are satisfied, the more relatedness needs will be desired.*

The basis for this proposition is that a person who is unable to find ways to use and develop his capacities looks to relationships as an alternative source of stimulation. Relationships provide a more concrete way for a person to receive stimulation than searching for one's own capabilities and for opportunities to utilize them.

Table 7-5 contains correlations for testing hypotheses derived from proposition 5. There were more statistically significant correlations than one would expect on the basis of chance alone, but the pattern of the correlations was not such as to support a general applicability of the proposition. All of the support was found for managers in the business organizations. This leads one to conjecture that when people with complex jobs are unable to utilize their abilities or learn, one reason is because they are blocked by other people. The desire for more open relationships would then be instrumental to obtaining opportunities to satisfy growth needs, not as substituting for growth needs.

Failure to find general support for proposition 5 does not represent as marked a departure from other research results as failure to find support for proposition 3. Most of the literature reviewed in connection with this hypothesis was based on indirect evidence or evidence where desires were inferred from particular behavior. Consequently, there is relatively little discrepancy between these findings and prior evidence.

THE MASLOW HYPOTHESES

Both empirical work and analysis of measuring instruments pointed to the tendency of Maslow's security, social, and esteem categories to converge on the subject of interpersonal relations. There are two kinds of hypotheses which seem to follow from Maslow's theory with respect to these needs. One kind of hypothesis follows from the prepotency assumption and has the general

Table 7-5. Correlations for Hypotheses based on Proposition 5

(The less growth needs are satisfied, the more relatedness needs will be desired.)

| | DESIRES | | | | | |
| | Managers | | | Employees | | |
GROWTH SATISFACTION	Superiors	Peers	Customers	Superiors	Peers	Customers
Manufacturing (n=34, 138)						
Job activities	-.57†	-.13		-.13	-.02	
Bank (n=60, 157)						
Job activities	-.31†	-.25*	.01	.04	.10	.10
Alpha House (n=57)						
House activities		.13				
Academic activities		-.02				
Beta House (n=46)						
House activities		.03				
Academic activities		-.11				

*p < .05   † p < .01

form that satisfaction of a lower-level need should be correlated with desires for higher order needs. The second kind of hypothesis also stems from the prepotency assumption applied to each of the lower-level needs. If a need ceases to be active after it is satisfied, as Maslow has said, then satisfaction of a need should be inversely correlated with desires for the same need. In this way Maslow's theory also may be seen as subsuming the simple-frustration hypothesis.

By using Schneider's instrument in the Bank study, it was possible to test hypotheses about the interpersonal aspects of Maslow's theory. Five specific hypotheses were articulated for testing:

1. The more security needs are satisfied, the more social needs will be desired.
2. The more social needs are satisfied, the more esteem needs will be desired.
3. The less security needs are satisfied, the more they will be desired.
4. The less social needs are satisfied, the more they will be desired.
5. The less esteem needs are satisfied, the more they will be desired.

Table 7-6 contains correlations for testing these hypotheses in the Bank setting. As a whole, the correlations show little consistent support for the hypotheses. All of them are positive among the manager group. There was a significant positive correlation between security satisfaction and social desires which provided support for hypothesis 1. The correlation between social satisfaction and esteem desire did not reach statistical significance although it was positive. The other positive correlations were directly opposed to

Table 7-6. Correlations Relevant to Maslow Interpersonal Needs

DESIRES

SATIS-FACTIONS	Managers (n=60)			Employees (n=157)		
	Security	Social	Esteem	Security	Social	Esteem
Security	.35	.26*	.20	−.02	.04	.00
Social	.27	.19	.13	.03	−.05	.03
Esteem	.02	.14	.23	.03	.05	.12

* p < .05
— p < .05, two-tailed test reversal of prediction
= p < .01, two-tailed test reversal of prediction

hypotheses 3-5. For the employee group, there were no significant relations and thus no support for any of the hypotheses.

The theoretical analysis suggested that there might be observable relationships between interpersonal needs measured by E.R.G. variables and the Maslow desires. Table 7-7 shows the correlations between specific relatedness satisfactions and the Maslow desires. Three out of nine correlations were significant in the predicted direction for both manager and employee groups. For the managers, peer satisfaction was inversely correlated with security desires and with social desires. Customer satisfaction was inversely correlated with social desires. For the employees, superiors satisfaction was inversely correlated with social and esteem desires. Customer satisfaction was inversely correlated with social desires. Table 7-8 contains the relationships which are complementary to those in Table 7-7; Maslow satisfactions were correlated with E.R.G. desires. There were no significant correlations in the predicted direction and one in the opposite direction.

Table 7-7.   Correlations between E.R.G. Relatedness Satisfactions and Maslow Interpersonal Desires

DESIRES

SATIS-FACTIONS	Managers (n=60)			Employees (n=157)		
	Security	Social	Esteem	Security	Social	Esteem
Superiors	.02	−.17*	.04	−.10	−.14*	−.20†
Peers	−.25*	−.24*	−.07	−.05	−.08	−.16
Customers	−.10	−.24*	−.06	.00	−.14†	−.04

* $p < .05$ † $p < .01$

The results reported here provide little in the way of encouragement for what Maslow's theory says about interpersonal needs. One question that might be raised concerns whether lower-level needs were adequately satisfied in order for security, social, and esteem needs to be operative in the way Maslow's theory says they should be. Our current measurement technology provides no direct way to answer this question, but the study results suggest that relatedness needs operated as expected. By this indirect means, one might rule out lack of basic need satisfaction as a reason for lack of support for the Maslow predictions. Another case might be made that the measurement properties of the Maslow scales were too poor for one

Table 7-8. Correlations between Maslow Interpersonal Satisfactions and E.R.G. Relatedness Desires

DESIRES

SATIS-FACTIONS	Managers (n=60)			Employees (n=157)		
	Superiors	Peers	Customers	Superiors	Peers	Customers
Security	.10	.12	−.03	−.12	−.03	−.10
Social	−.03	.05	−.06	−.10	−.11	−.09
Esteem	.27	.12	−.08	−.03	.03	−.04

— $p < .05$, reversal of prediction

to take the tests of the Maslow hypotheses seriously. If this were true, why should relationships between relatedness satisfactions and the Maslow desires be found to behave in expected ways? On balance it seems fair to conclude that the relatedness concept deals more adequately with interpersonal needs than Maslow's security, social, and esteem categories.

CHRONIC RELATEDNESS DESIRES AND RELATEDNESS SATISFACTION

E.R.G. theory attempts to deal not only with how satisfaction affects desires but also with how chronic desires affect satisfaction. Three studies in the present series provided an opportunity to test hypotheses derived from proposition 9, which are:

P9a. In highly satisfying relationships, there is no differential relatedness satisfaction as a function of chronic relatedness desires.
P9b. In normal relationships, persons very high and very low on chronic relatedness desires tend to obtain lower satisfaction than persons with moderate desires.
P9c. In highly dissatisfying relationships, the higher the chronic relatedness desires, the more relatedness satisfaction.

Recruitment interviews were an attempt to develop access to the

three different states of relatedness satisfaction.[1] Adolescent Lab
provided a setting where relatedness needs were expected to be highly
satisfied. Boys School was a setting where one might expect an
average level of satisfaction to be obtained.

Table 7-9 contains the mean relatedness satisfaction scores for
three levels of chronic relatedness needs in each of three recruitment interviews. In the worst interviews, those persons with high
relatedness needs reported greater satisfaction than those with low
relatedness needs. The relationship between chronic need level and
satisfaction for the worst interview was monotonically increasing
and thereby provides support for proposition 9c. There were no significant differences between persons of different need levels in the
satisfaction they obtained in the best and average interviews. The
findings with respect to the best interviews also provide support for
proposition 9a while the findings with regard to the average interview do not support proposition 9b.

It is apparent from Table 7-9 that the quality of the interviews,
which was an interactive phenomenon depending on both the inter-
viewer and the candidate, was much more potent in determining
need satisfaction than the candidate's relatedness needs. Even
though the satisfaction differences between need levels were not
significant in the best interviews, satisfaction was greatest for those
of moderate needs.

**Table 7-9.   Mean Relatedness Satisfaction by Chronic Need Level
and Interview Type for Recruitment Study**

| | *INTERVIEW TYPE* | | |
CHRONIC NEED LEVEL	*Worst* ($n=112$)	*Average* ($n=112$)	*Best* ($n=112$)
Low ($n=29$)	1.90	8.10	10.14
Medium ($n=56$)	2.12	7.72	10.49
High ($n=27$)	4.89	7.63	10.15

$F_{\text{Overall}} = 65.99, \ p < .01$
$F_{\text{Best vs. Worst}} = 668.7, \ p < .01$
$F_{\text{Low Worst vs. High Worst}} = 10.93, \ p < .01$

[1] The theoretical analysis and data from the recruitment interviews represent
a reconceptualization and reanalysis of the material in Alderfer and McCord
(1970).

Table 7-10 contains the mean satisfaction scores for three different levels of chronic relatedness needs from the Adolescent Lab. Desire and satisfaction measures were obtained for both faculty and peers. None of the mean differences in satisfaction between need levels were significant, but in each case those persons of moderate needs reported greater satisfaction than those of high or low needs. The findings from Adolescent Lab are consistent with what might be expected if proposition 9a were correct. However, one cannot claim direct support for the hypothesis because that would be committing the error of accepting the null hypothesis (Blalock, 1960). The differences might have failed to reach statistical significance because measures were not sensitive enough to detect real differences with the given sample size.

Table 7-10. Mean Relatedness Satisfaction by Chronic Need Level in Adolescent Lab

CHRONIC NEED FOR FACULTY TRUST	Relatedness satisfaction with staff	CHRONIC NEED FOR STUDENT TRUST	Relatedness satisfaction with group
Low (n=32)	6.57	Low (n=33)	4.29
Medium (n=28)	8.20	Medium (n=28)	7.13
High (n=23)	5.96	High (n=22)	6.53

No significant differences

Table 7-11 shows the mean satisfaction scores for students from Boys School of three levels of chronic relatedness needs. At each time interval from when the chronic needs were measured, those with moderate needs reported the greatest satisfaction. But the number of people from whom satisfaction measures were taken after seven months was approximately twice the number after two months. This resulted in a more powerful statistical test and produced statistical significance among the need levels at the second assessment while it did not at the first measurement. If the Boys School setting can be viewed as providing average relatedness satisfaction, then these results can be viewed as giving support to proposition 9b.

Data from the three settings taken together provide some support for proposition 9 and very little that is inconsistent with the reasoning of that proposition. The only data point that is slightly inconsistent with the proposition occurred when the people with lowest chronic needs obtained the highest need satisfaction from the average re-cruitment interview. On the other hand, without committing the

Table 7-11.   Mean Peer Satisfaction by Chronic Need Level in Boys School at Two Time Intervals

CHRONIC NEED FOR STUDENT TRUST	After 2 months	After 7 months
Low	2.38 ($n=39$)	2.26 ($n=64$)
Medium	3.54 ($n=26$)	3.64 ($n=50$)
High	2.40 ($n=20$)	2.38 ($n=49$)
	differences not significant	$F_{\text{Overall}}=7.23, p<.01*$ $F_{\text{Medium vs. Low and High}}=6.76, p<.05*$

* F values adjusted to reflect sampling from 70 per cent of population

error of accepting the null hypothesis, one cannot claim that the data from Adolescent Lab support proposition 9a.   A similar approach would result in disconfirmation of proposition 9b based on the two months' data from Boys School.

SUMMARY AND CONCLUSIONS

This chapter was devoted to reporting on the relationships be-tween satisfactions and desires for interpersonal needs.   One set of results concerned the support for three E.R.G. propositions.   Two of these, numbers three and five, received very little consistent or general support from the data.   For proposition 3, we argued that the evidence from other research was too strong to warrant dropping it from the theory based on the current findings, while for proposi-tion 5 we could find little reason to retain it in the theory based on current or previous research.   Proposition 4 received strong general support, but the data also indicated several important ways to change and elaborate it. Evidence from both static and dynamic data and from several organizations supported the revised notion that the sign of the relationship between relatedness satisfaction and desire depends on the absolute level of relatedness satisfaction. In relatively dissatisfying situations, satisfaction is inversely related to desire. In relatively satisfying situations, satisfaction is positively related to desire. Moreover, the strength of the relationship between satisfaction and desire may depend upon the group position of the person being satisfied and toward whom he is relating. For leaders, significant others outside a group, such as their boss or a customer, may be as crucial or more crucial than these same people would be for members inside the group.

Very little support was found for any of the Maslow conceptions concerning interpersonal needs. At the same time, considerable support was given to the E.R.G. conceptualization. Consequently, we would conclude that the E.R.G. approach to studying relatedness needs offers an improvement over Maslow's theory in the area of interpersonal relations.

Several findings also provided support for the E.R.G. approach to how chronic relatedness needs affect relatedness satisfaction. Due to methodological limitations in the studies, however, the whole of proposition 9 cannot be viewed as receiving quite the convergent support that was given to the revised version of proposition 4.

Chapter 8

GROWTH DESIRES

W<small>HEN</small> Maslow (1943) initially proposed his prepotency theory of human needs, the self-actualization need was hardly an accepted concept among behavioral scientists, but succeeding years have seen greater interest develop in this and related ideas. Psychoanalytically oriented personality theorists such as Fromm (1947) and Sullivan (1953) worked toward expanding analytic concepts to include notions such as a productive orientation or the tendency toward health. Laboratory oriented psychologists became concerned with exploration, manipulation, and curiosity (Harlow, 1953; Montgomery, 1954; Fiske and Maddi, 1968). Robert White (1959, 1960, 1963) presented a series of papers in which he united the evidence from these different sources by introducing the notion of competence motivation. The concept of growth needs owes much to these writers.

Growth needs were postulated to account for the frequently observed facts which indicate that persons seem to interact with their environments so they can use their abilities and learn. Most persons live in more than one ecological environment. Each of us faces several physical settings in which a stable set of people carry out some regular pattern of activities. Specific growth needs are defined in terms of different environments such as homes, jobs, and hobbies.

Among researchers in the field of organizational psychology, there has been disagreement about the utility of concepts like growth desires. Strauss (1963), for example, raised questions about what he called the "universality of the desire for self-actualization." He proposed that such needs might be higher among the academicians who write about workers than among the workers themselves. As a consequence, the investigators might be projecting their own needs onto the workers when they postulate self-actualization or growth motives. Unless the view is taken that the presence of growth desires is perfectly correlated with social class, then the question raised by Strauss can most parsimoniously be handled through the operation of chronic individual differences in growth desires. To assume that all people have some desire for growth is not the same as saying that all people have a high degree of desire for growth. E.R.G. theory takes the former but not the latter position.

Although Maslow's need for self-actualization has much in common with the E.R.G. need for growth, there are some differences at the conceptual level. Growth needs arise from viewing the person as an open system interacting with his environments. Inputs from the environment provide stimuli for a person to develop certain abilities and opportunities to use certain capacities. When the environment changes, then the nature of growth desires may change. Maslow's concept places less emphasis on the differentiating affects of the environment. The flavor of his concept is that of a person at birth with certain potentials; if he faces a favorable environment, then his potentials will be realized. He will become a self-actualized man.

Maslow's approach was sharply criticized by Berkowitz (1964) who interpreted the concept of self-actualization to mean that a person should seek his own ends without regard for the needs of others. Berkowitz (1964) probably misunderstood Maslow's views, but the way that the concept was formulated aided misunderstanding. The emphasis on individual environment interaction, which lies at the heart of the growth conceptualization, differs in degree only with Maslow's formulation. But this difference may serve to diminish the latent flavor of self-aggrandizement which some critics of self-actualization concept have felt.

In the present chapter, we shall deal with several aspects of growth needs: (1) Testing hypotheses from E.R.G. theory which predict how growth desires are affected by various need satisfactions, and (2) testing hypotheses from E.R.G. propositions which predict how chronic growth needs affect growth satisfaction.

E.R.G. HYPOTHESES FROM SATISFACTION TO DESIRE

The first proposition predicting to variations in the strength of growth desires is:

> P6. *The more relatedness needs are satisfied, the more growth needs will be desired.*

The basic notion behind this proposition is that a person is more likely to become aware of and attempt to fulfill his potentials as a person when he is supported by open and trusting relationships with significant others in his life. The uncertainty and psychological threat which growth always entails will be more readily sought by a person when he knows that he can mutually share his thoughts and feelings with others. The general spirit of this proposition is similar to Maslow's theory, except that it does not presuppose lower-level need gratification.

Table 8-1 presents the static correlations from testing hypotheses based on proposition 6 in various organization settings. Two of the

Table 8-1.   Static Correlations for Hypotheses Based on Proposition 6

(The more relatedness needs are satisfied, the more growth needs will be desired.)

RELATEDNESS SATISFACTION	*Managers*	*DESIRES*		*Employees*
Manufacturing ($n=34$, 138)				
Superiors	–.13			–.26
Peers	–.17			–.18
Bank ($n=60$, 157)				
Superiors	–.15			–.13
Peers	–.26			–.06
Customers	–.09			.00
		House	*Academic*	
Alpha House ($n=57$)				
Peers		.28*	–.01	
Beta House ($n=46$)				
Peers		.21	–.21	

* $p<.05$
— significant in the opposite direction at .05 or less

correlations were in the predicted direction, and one of these was significant, while two other correlations were significant in the opposite direction by a two-tailed test. None of the other correlations were significant. Data from the business organizations provide no support at all for the proposition, while the fraternity data provide some support for it. There was some consistency among the fraternity findings. In both houses, positive correlations between peer satisfaction and growth desires were observed for desires for growth from house activities but not for desires for growth from academic activities. Taken together, these results suggest that proposition 6 may be valid under quite special conditions, rather than being completely general.

Table 8-2 presents dynamic correlations relevant to testing hypotheses from proposition 6.[1] Rather strong support for the proposition was found in the data collected during the latter half of Adult Lab, and some support was found in the data taken from Boys School. These findings increase the general empirical support for proposition 6 but also underline the need for specifying the conditions under which it is valid.

Table 8-2. Dynamic Correlations Relevant to Proposition 6

Relatedness satisfactions		*Growth desires*
Adult Lab ($n=46$)		
t_1, t_2	Superiors	.01
		(−.02)
	Peers	−.09
		(−.03)
t_2, t_3	Superiors	.20
		(.33)†
	Peers	.32†
		(.23)*
Boys School ($n=77$)		
	Peers	.18*
		(.16)

* $p < .05$ † $p < .01$

[1] The procedure for computing raw and corrected dynamic correlations was the same here as reported in Chapter 7.

All of the support for proposition 6 was found in settings where human learning was a primary reason for their existence. The fraternities, Adult Lab, and Boys School were all institutions devoted to general goals of education and human development. Among the business settings where such a goal was not articulated at all or was of secondary priority, there was no support at all for the proposition. At the fraternities, where it was possible to measure one set of growth desires directly relevant to the setting and another set indirectly relevant, support for proposition 6 was found only for those growth desires directly relevant to the setting. In Adult Lab, where relatedness satisfaction increased with time, strong support for proposition 6 was found in the latter portion of the lab when relatedness satisfaction was highest. Greater support for proposition 6 was found in Alpha House than in Beta House, even though the difference in correlations was small. As noted earlier, Alpha House had higher overall relatedness satisfaction than Beta House.

These results suggest that proposition 6 is most likely to be valid when the mean values of both relatedness and growth satisfactions are relatively high. It neither need is very satisfied then, proposition 6 seems unlikely to apply. The fact that support for the proposition was found in settings other than the human relations laboratory suggests that growth satisfaction may weigh more heavily than relatedness satisfaction in determining when increasing the satisfaction of relatedness needs increases desires for growth.

The second E.R.G. proposition which predicts variations in the strength of growth desires is:

P7. The more growth needs are satisfied, the more they will be desired.

This proposition captures the idea that growth is intrinsically satisfying. As a person becomes aware of a new aspect of himself, he develops a new capability, he attempts to use it, to try it out, and to see how it fits with his more fully integrated aspects. At the same time, a person faces a constant source of stimulation from his environment. When the environmental stimulation is consistent with already established capabilities, then it provides a person with the opportunity to use his abilities. If the environment is full of challenge and change, then it makes demands on the person to develop additional capacities if he is to be meaningfully and fully integrated with the world in which he lives. A person moves among environments, this alteration provides another source for integration and differentiation. The capacities developed in one setting may be tried in another environment. The integration achieved in one setting may be challenged by new stimuli in another environment.

In Maslow's earlier work (1943; 1954), he did not take a position regarding the impact of satisfaction on self-actualization needs. However, in his later work (1962, p. 31) he did say that the more growth is obtained, the more it will be desired. Thus, proposition 7 is in essential agreement with Maslow's later views.

Table 8-3 shows the static correlations for testing hypotheses based on proposition 7, and Table 8-4 shows the results of dynamic

Table 8-3. Static Correlations for Hypotheses Based on Proposition 7

(The more growth needs are satisfied, the more they will be desired.)

GROWTH DESIRES

SATISFACTION	*Managers*		*Employees*
Manufacturing ($n=34$, 138)			
Work	-.33		-.22
Bank ($n=60$, 157)			
Work	-.11		-.06

	House	*Academic*
Alpha House ($n=57$)		
House	.60†	.23*
Academic	.06	.47†
Beta House ($n=46$)		
House	.51†	-.19
Academic	-.03	.28*

* $p<.05$
† $p<.01$
— significant in the opposite direction by two-tailed test

correlations testing hypotheses from proposition 7. Immediately apparent from these findings is the contrast between the strong support provided for proposition 7 by the fraternity studies as compared with the lack of support from the business settings. In Alpha

House, growth satisfaction from house activities was positively correlated with growth desires from house activities and with growth desires from academic activities. Growth satisfaction from academic activities was positively related to growth desires from academic activities. In Beta House, growth satisfaction from house activities was positively related to growth desires from house activities, and growth satisfaction from academic activities was positively related to growth desires from academic activities. Thus, in Alpha House support was found for proposition 7 not only within specific needs but also between the specific needs of house and academic activities. At Manufacturing, however, the signs of the correlations were opposite from the predicted direction, and at Bank the correlations were essentially zero.

The dynamic correlations taken at Adult Lab and Boys School were all positive, although it was only the Boys School results which reached statistical significance. At Adult Lab, the correlations for the second half of the week were higher than during the first half.

Table 8-4. Dynamic Correlations Relevant to Proposition 7

Adult Lab ($n=46$)

t_1, t_2	.11
	(.08)
t_2, t_3	.17
	(.16)

Boys School ($n=77$)

Academic activities	.22*
	(.22)*

* $p < .05$

It would appear from these results that growth satisfaction is positively related to growth desires when growth satisfaction is relatively high but not when it is relatively low. Moreover, the negative correlations from Manufacturing suggest that growth satisfaction may actually be negatively related to growth desires at low levels of growth satisfaction. To test this possibility, nearly equal groups of respondents were formed according to satisfaction level for the settings where static data had been collected. The mean desire score for each satisfaction level was then computed. These results are shown in Table 8-5.

At Manufacturing, the mean growth-desire score for each satisfaction level was monotonically *decreasing* for each succeeding level of growth satisfaction except for the most satisfied group. Growth desire increased from the second most-satisfied group to the most-satisfied group. At Bank, the mean growth-desire score for each satisfaction level was monotonically *decreasing* for the three lowest satisfaction levels and monotonically *increasing* for the three highest satisfaction levels. For both of the specific needs in the combined fraternity analysis, growth desires were monotonically increasing for all levels of satisfaction.[1]

Table 8-5. Growth Desire Means for Different Growth Satisfaction Levels

	MANUFACTURING			BANK	
n	*Growth satisfaction*	*Growth desire*	*n*	*Growth satisfaction*	*Growth desire*
28	7.39	8.14	39	6.52	3.84
27	19.04	7.92	35	12.14	1.19
28	27.54	7.04	31	14.55	.19
30	35.45	4.13	35	16.46	2.32
31	42.69	3.26	41	19.12	2.51
32	52.43	5.84	46	21.28	3.31

COMBINED FRATERNITIES

	Growth from house satisfaction	*Growth from house desire*		*Growth from academics satisfaction*	*Growth from academics desire*
n			*n*		
22	1.41	8.63	25	2.56	13.08
28	4.68	13.36	25	6.72	15.24
29	8.88	13.57	26	9.62	15.62
24	11.75	14.67	27	12.12	16.89

[1] The only place where the satisfaction or desire scale values are comparable is with respect to the fraternity studies. Between Manufacturing and Bank, different numbers of items and different wording of items were employed. Consequently, direct comparison of satisfaction levels between organizations was not possible.

From these results, a revision of proposition 7 seems in order. The relationship between growth satisfaction and desire depends on the absolute level of growth satisfaction. For low levels of growth satisfaction, the more growth satisfaction, the less growth desire. For high levels of growth satisfaction, the more growth satisfaction, the more growth desires. Perhaps at very low levels of satisfaction, a person is troubled by monotony or stimulus deprivation while at higher levels of satisfaction he wants to grow in order to utilize the opportunities that he faces more fully.

Elaboration of proposition 7 might also be considered in relation to the operation of specific growth needs. There was a difference between the two fraternities in the degree to which growth satisfaction from house activities was correlated with desires for academic growth. At Alpha House, the correlation was significantly positive, while at Beta House the correlation was insignificantly negative. The difference between these two correlations was significant at the .05 level. From other data collected from the fraternities, we know that the tension between house and academic activities was less for members of Alpha House than for members of Beta House (Alderfer and Lodahl, 1970). Perhaps the degree to which growth satisfaction in one setting affects growth desires in another setting depends on the degree to which the first setting encourages behavior which could lead to growth satisfaction in the second setting. In neither house was academic growth satisfaction related to desires for growth from house activities. While the fraternity life could aid a member in his academic work, it seems unlikely that the academic setting would be encouraging of growth from fraternity activities.

CHRONIC GROWTH DESIRES AND GROWTH SATISFACTION

According to E.R.G. theory, chronic growth desires also affect a person's tendency to obtain growth satisfaction, depending on the kind of setting he faces. Proposition 10a states:

> P10a. *In challenging discretionary settings, the higher chronic growth desires, the more growth satisfaction.*

This E.R.G. hypothesis, which deals with the impact of chronic desires on satisfaction, presupposes a time delay between the desire-measurement and desire-obtained satisfaction. The time delay allows a person to operate on his environment so that he can do the things which bring him growth satisfaction.

Two of the organization settings studied provided an opportunity for chronic growth desires to be measured prior to the beginning of a series of challenging and discretionary activities. Two weeks prior to Adolescent Lab, measures of chronic growth desires were taken, and then near the end of the laboratory, measures of growth satisfaction from the laboratory were taken. Prior to the startings of school, measures of chronic growth desires were taken at Boys School, and then two months into the school year, measures of growth satisfaction from academic activities were obtained.

The data bearing on testing hypotheses based on proposition 10*a* are shown in Table 8-6. Both settings provided data which supported the hypotheses. Growth satisfaction increased monotonically as a function of chronic growth desires.

Table 8-6. **Means for Hypotheses based on Proposition 10a**

(In challenging discretionary settings, the higher chronic growth desires, the more growth satisfaction.)

Chronic growth desire	*Mean growth satisfaction*
Adolescent Lab (time: 2 weeks)	
Low ($n=33$)	2.59
Medium ($n=23$)	2.90
High ($n=27$)	3.03
Boys School (time: 2 months)	
Low ($n=34$)	1.26
Medium ($n=33$)	3.06
High ($n=34$)	3.12

$p < .05$

Putting together the results from testing hypotheses based on proposition 7 with those from testing hypotheses from proposition 10*a*, one can find support for what was defined in chapter 2 as the growth enrichment cycle. In those settings where relatively high growth satisfaction is possible, the higher a person's chronic growth desires the more growth satisfaction he tends to obtain. The more growth satisfaction he obtains, the more growth he desires.

Summary and Conclusions The subject of this chapter was growth desires, how various need satisfactions affect growth desires and how chronic growth desires affect the tendency to obtain growth satisfaction. We reported the results of investigations which tested hypotheses concerning how relatedness satisfaction was related to growth desires and how growth satisfaction was related to growth desires. The outcome of these results was both to support the general notions contained in propositions 6 and 7 and to suggest important changes in them by specifying more precisely the conditions under which they would tend to lead to valid predictions.

When both relatedness and growth satisfactions were relatively high, then satisfaction of relatedness needs was more likely to be associated with desires for growth. When growth satisfaction was relatively low, then growth satisfaction was inversely related to growth desires. But when growth satisfaction was relatively high, then growth satisfaction was positively associated with growth desires.

Our results also suggested that growth satisfaction in one setting was more likely to affect growth desires in another environment if behavior in the first setting could facilitate growth satisfaction in the second setting.

Data bearing on the impact of individual differences in chronic growth desires supported the hypothesis that persons with higher growth needs tend to obtain more growth satisfaction in challenging discretionary settings than persons with lower chronic growth needs. Combining the results pertinent to the relationship of growth satisfaction to growth desires with those relevant to the relationship of chronic growth desires to growth satisfaction supported the concept of a growth enrichment cycle. In settings rich with opportunities for growth, those who want more get more and vice versa.

The material covered in this chapter does not represent any new areas of major difference with Maslow's theory. Modifications in E.R.G. theory which were suggested by these data could also be suggested for Maslow's theory. Support found for E.R.G. theory in these areas might also be viewed as support for Maslow's views. A minor difference lies with the way that E.R.G. theory can identify specific growth needs while Maslow's theory does not. This difference was supported by the results shown in this chapter. All of the support found for $P6$ and $P7$ argues against the universslity of the simple frustration hypothesis, which does not allow for positive relationships between satisfaction and desire.

Chapter 9

CONCLUSIONS AND IMPLICATIONS

THE major purpose of this chapter is to take stock by drawing together the conclusions reached at various points in the book, raising questions that should be raised about these conclusions, revising the model based on the data, and drawing implications from the empirical results and the theory. At various points in presenting the data, changes in the E.R.G. model were proposed, and at other times, the data were interpreted to support the model. Now we shall attempt to draw all of these separate statements together in an effort to formulate the best possible model in light of the data now collected. It will also be a time to review the methodological problems involved in research of this kind and to note the qualifications that should be added to an assessment of results of this type. Questions with regard to how E.R.G. theory compares to other views and how it might complement process theories of motivation will be discussed. The series of studies reported here hardly exhaust the range of possible research projects that might be carried out to test, elaborate, or revise E.R.G. theory. The present studies can provide perspective for thinking about future investigations. Finally, the present work also contains implications for action if one should wish to utilize the present results as a basis for designing or redesigning motivational systems.

REFORMULATION OF THE THEORY

During the course of presenting the results of testing E.R.G. propositions, a number of different kinds of changes in the theory were proposed. One kind of change was concerned with how the specific needs *within* each of the broad categories were related to each other. Prior to the current investigation there were no statements in E.R.G. theory to deal with such questions. A second kind of change was concerned with specifying more precisely the conditions under which certain of the propositions were valid and thereby changing the statement of the propositions themselves. The third kind of change concerned raising questions about certain propositions for which there was little, if any, consistent empirical support.

The Relation of Specific Needs within Categories

When it was possible to obtain measures of satisfaction and desire of more than one specific need within a category, it became apparent that not all satisfactions had the same size correlation with desires within the same category. Generally speaking, satisfaction of a need correlated most strongly with desire for the need itself (either positively or negatively). But beyond this generalization, there were noticeable patterns among the correlations relating satisfaction and desire between different specific needs. As a result of observing the pattern of correlations between satisfaction and desire among the different categories, it was possible to induce a number of tentative explanatory mechanisms to predict the degree to which satisfaction of specific needs within a category would be related to desires of other needs within the same category. These mechanisms varied according to the need categories.

Existence Needs Satisfaction and desire were more highly correlated among different existence needs that shared a common modality than among different existence needs which did not share a common modality. One such common modality would be financial. Different existence needs which were financially based (e.g., pay and fringe benefits) showed higher correlations between satisfaction and desire than they did with an existence need based on fear of bodily harm.

Relatedness Needs The strength of the relationship between satisfaction and desire for varying significant others seemed to depend upon the group position of the person who was receiving the satis-faction and the person with whom a relationship existed. Managers (who were group leaders) tended to show higher correlations be-tween satisfaction and desire for significant others outside the work group than employees (who were group members).

Growth Needs Although the amount of data on which compari-sons could be based was limited it seemed that the strength of rela-tionship between satisfaction and desire of different growth needs depended on the degree of which the on-going behavior patterns of two settings were compatible. When the norms in one setting sup-ported growth in another setting, then growth satisfaction in one setting was related to growth desires in another setting. The frater-nity which had the least split between house and academic goals showed a positive correlation between growth satisfaction from house activities and growth desires from academic activities. The fraternity with the greater split between house and academic activities did not show a similar correlation.

Conditions under which Propositions are Valid

There were two kinds of changes made in the basic E.R.G. propo-sitions. In one instance, two propositions were changed from linear to curvilinear forms. In the other case, the absolute value of certain satisfactions were proposed to set conditions under which one frus-tration-regression and one satisfaction-progression proposition held.

The initial formulation of proposition 4 concerning the relation-ship between relatedness satisfaction and desire proposed an inverse relationship. However, data from the human relations laboratory indicated that, when relatedness satisfaction was highest, the relation-ship between satisfaction and desire was positive. Re-examination of the static data indicated that in two settings the most satisfied groups showed higher desires than the second most satisfied groups, even though throughout the rest of the satisfaction range, desire decreased monotonically as satisfaction increased. Therefore, pro-position 4 was modified to state that under conditions of low satis-faction, relatedness satisfaction was inversely related to desire, but under conditions of high satisfaction, relatedness satisfaction was positively related to desire.

A similar change was proposed for growth needs. In this case, the change was to recognize that under certain circumstances, growth satisfaction was inversely related to desires. Proposition 7 was modified to state that under conditions of low satisfaction, growth satisfaction was inversely related to desire, but under conditions of high satisfaction, growth satisfaction was positively related to desire.

Anticipating the introduction of curvilinear forms for relatedness and growth needs, we presented the mean values of pay desires for succeeding levels of pay satisfaction in Chapter 6. Unlike the results for relatedness and growth needs, the pay desire means were monotonically decreasing for each succeeding satisfaction level. From these data, there was no reason to consider changing proposition 1 in the same way that propositions 4 and 7 were changed. Although the range of pay covered in the present studies went from less than $4,000 to more than $40,000 annually, there was no empirical reason to rule out the possibility that the curve might turn upward for even higher values of satisfaction. But the current data offer no reason to believe it would.

Data collected to test proposition 3 concerning the relationship between relatedness satisfaction and existence desires indicated that this proposition had some general support, but it did not seem to hold under all circumstances. Examination of the conditions under which it was supported in comparison to those under which it was not led to a proposed modification. Under conditions of low existence and relatedness satisfaction, relatedness satisfaction was inversely related to existence desires.

An analogous change was proposed for proposition 6 which dealt with the relationship between relatedness satisfaction and growth desires. This proposition, too, received general support but not under all circumstances. In this case, the support seemed to be found most frequently when the satisfaction of both relatedness and growth needs was relatively high. This led to a modification of proposition 6. Under conditions of high relatedness and growth satisfaction, relatedness satisfaction was positively related to growth desires.

Questionable Propositions

Two propositions in the theory received very little general support from the data collected in the various organizations. The first was concerned with the relationship between existence satisfaction and relatedness desires, and the second was concerned with the relationship between growth satisfaction and relatedness desires. In the first case, data from other investigations, especially the food deprivation research with humans, would be inconsistent with abandoning the proposition. But in the second case, there was little in the data from the current investigations or from other work which made a strong case for retaining the proposition.

Further Theoretical Issues

These changes have raised some general theoretical issues at the same time that they have altered the kinds of empirical predictions one would make from E.R.G. theory. The frustration-regression postulate appears to apply only to relatedness and existence needs but not to growth needs. The satisfaction-progression postulate seems to apply primarily to relatedness and growth needs but not to existence needs. Why should relatedness satisfaction be inversely related to existence desires at low levels of satisfaction of both needs? A person whose relatedness needs are severely frustrated probably lives in fear of losing contact with significant others and thereby losing the relationship entirely. His quest for material factors serves a double purpose under these circumstances. Material objects remain a way to get something out of the relationship even superficially. Seeking material gratification also provides a way to express anger indirectly.

Why should relatedness satisfaction be positively related to growth desires at high levels of satisfaction of both needs? Because relatedness needs involve dealing with other people, their satisfaction is often intimately related to self-awareness. Most people have mixed feelings about increasing their self-awareness. On the one hand, they may want to know, but on the other hand, they may fear what they might learn. High relatedness satisfaction provides support for the seeking self-awareness, while high growth satisfaction provides stimulation for increasing learning.

Why do the relatedness and growth needs show curvilinear relations between satisfaction and desire? When a relationship between people stands on the downward sloping part of the relatedness satisfaction–desire curve, there is probably some question about the long-term tenability of the relationship. Perhaps one or both parties would terminate the relationship if he could. When a human relationship stands on the upward sloping part of the relatedness satisfaction–desire curve, there is probably no danger of terminating the relationship but only opportunities to obtain mutual satisfaction. When a person is experiencing the downward sloping part of the growth satisfaction–desire curve he is probably under-stimulated and suffering from monotony and boredom. At the upward sloping portion of the curve, he is confronting opportunities to utilize his capabilities and develop his talents.

The changes that have been discussed so far provide the major directions for revising E.R.G. theory. Little in the empirical data offered any reason to consider changing the basic category system. In general, the three categories of human needs seemed to provide a fruitful way to think about the major wants of persons. In general, the propositions which dealt with the relationship between chronic desires and satisfaction were consistent with the data when they were tested. There was little reason to consider changing propositions 8 to 10 at this time, and there was data to support their continued viability.

At this time, therefore, the version of E.R.G. theory which is most consistent with the empirical data contains the following propositions:

P1.   The less existence needs are satisfied, the more they will be desired.

P2.   (Revised) When both existence and relatedness needs are relatively dissatisfied, the less relatedness needs are satisfied, the more existence needs will be desired.

P4.   (Revised) When relatedness needs are relatively dissatisfied, the less relatedness needs are satisfied, the more they will be desired; when relatedness needs are relatively satisfied, the more relatedness needs are satisfied, the more they will be desired.

P6.   (Revised) When both relatedness and growth needs are relatively satisfied, the more relatedness needs are satisfied, the more growth needs will be desired.

P7.   (Revised) When growth needs are relatively dissatisfied, the less growth needs are satisfied, the more they will be desired; when growth needs are relatively satisfied, the more growth needs are satisfied, the more they will be desired.

P8a. When existence materials are scarce, then the higher the chronic existence desires, the less the existence satisfaction.

P8b. When existence materials are not scarce, then there will be no differential existence satisfaction as a function of chronic existence desires.

P9a. In highly satisfying relationships, there is no differential relatedness satisfaction as a function of chronic relatedness desires.

P9b. In normal relationships, persons very high and very low on chronic relatedness desires tend to obtain lower satisfaction than persons with moderate desires.

P9c. In highly dissatisfying relationships, then, the higher chronic relatedness desires, the more relatedness satisfaction.

P10a. In challenging discretionary settings, then, the higher chronic growth desires, the more growth satisfaction.

P10b. In nonchallenging, nondiscretionary settings, there will be no differential growth satisfaction as a function of chronic growth desires.

Two derivations from the original E.R.G. propositions were also outlined in Chapter 2. One concerned the existence deficiency cycle, and the other concerned the growth enrichment cycle. Data from the present investigations dealt directly with only the growth enrichment cycle and provided support for it. No data were obtained to test the existence deficiency cycle.

METHODOLOGICAL ISSUES

All of the preceding statements rest on the assumption that the data reported were collected in such a way as to make the foregoing interpretations viable. From the outset, we alerted the reader to possible limitations in the kind of investigation undertaken. At this point, we address a number of key methodological issues in order to see the degree to which various methodological questions might limit the confidence one might place in the results obtained. The range of issues cover causality, questionnaire properties, curvilinear results, and generality of the findings.

Causality

None of the results reported from the various organizations was taken from an experiment. All of the data were correlational, whether the correlations were static or dynamic. Consequently, at no time could one be completely sure of the causal direction influencing the observed associations between variables. For this particular investigation, however, these observations do not end the subject of causality.

The special contribution of dynamic correlations (as opposed to static correlations alone) is that the use of correlations between change scores strengthens the case that an observed correlation between two variables was not the product of some third variable being spuriously correlated with both (Vroom, 1966). Not all of the E.R.G. propositions were tested by dynamic as well as static correlations, but all of the revised propositions (4, 6, 7) concerning relatedness and growth needs were based on the convergence of static and dynamic correlations. The fact that the static and dynamic correlations tend to agree also provides support for the assumption that changes in satisfaction produce more or less instantaneous changes in desire. If this assumption is true, it also means that the use of static correlations is a valid, though not maximally rigorous, way to test hypotheses from the theory.

In presenting the concept of need satisfaction in contrast to desire, we underlined the idea that satisfaction is rooted in a person's external world, while desire is a purely subjective state. The data showing how various satisfactions were correlated with demographic and organizational variables supported the case that satisfactions could be tied to external events and were not solely a function of the vicissitudes of a person's subjective states. These facts strengthen the *logical* case that can be made for satisfaction preceding desire even though neither the static nor dynamic correlations can firmly establish the *empirical* case for satisfaction being causally prior to desire.

The data from Adolescent Lab and Boys School showed that chronic desires measured in advance of events tend to be associated with satisfactions obtained from those events in predictable ways. E.R.G. propositions make a case that chronic desires affect satisfactions with a time delay while a person does or does not do things which might bring satisfaction to him. The theory also states that satisfactions affect desires essentially instantaneously. The data we have reported are generally consistent with these views of causality but have not established an unambiguous empirical case for them.

Questionnaire Properties

The E.R.G. questionnaires were designed purposefully to avoid certain methodological pitfalls which might produce spurious correlations among variables. The details of these design factors were given in Chapter 4. However, just because these methodological problems were anticipated in advance does not mean that the adjustments made to cope with them had the desired affect. The data taken from the various settings does provide an opportunity to see if certain methodological artifacts were operating.

Suppose, for example, a respondent wished to appear consistent in his behavior. As a consequence he may decide to say that he wants more of anything that he is not adequately obtaining. This kind of heuristic would produce negative correlations between satisfaction and desire for all needs. The results show positive as well as negative correlations between satisfaction and desire for various needs. One might take the argument a step further, however, and note that some kinds of organizational settings were more likely to show negative correlations while others were more likely to show positive correlations. Perhaps response sets were organization specific. But this view is not consistent with the observations either. Perhaps the strongest contrary evidence comes from the fraternities. In these organizations, there were positive correlations between growth satisfaction and desire and between relatedness satisfaction and growth desire. There were negative correlations between relatedness satisfaction and desire and between existence satisfaction and desire.

Curvilinearity

Two of the major propositions in E.R.G. theory were changed from linear to curvilinear forms based on data from different organizations, and on the convergence of static and dynamic correlations. A recent investigation by Dachler and Hulin (1969) raised some questions about the possibility of curvilinearity being produced by response bias characteristics in Likert scale items and importance ratings. Since both Likert scale items and importance ratings were employed in the present study, the relevance of their methodological points should be addressed in the context of the data reported here.

Dachler and Hulin (1969) reported that V-shaped curves were found for satisfaction and importance items on many different topics when both scales utilized a Likert format. But when JDI cumulative-point adjective check list satisfaction scales were plotted against importance ratings, the V-shaped relations were not observed. They argued that the item by item V curves were primarily artifactual functions of the measurement scales. With this point, we would offer little disagreement. An important question, however, is whether their results also imply that the curvilinear findings reported in the present studies were also artifactual. A number of elements in the present investigation tend to rule out artifactual explanations for these curvilinear forms.

First, curvilinear forms did not apply to all of the needs. They were found for relatedness and growth needs but not for existence needs. Second, the minimum point on the curves rarely occurred at the mid-point of the satisfaction distribution as it would have if the observed effect was artifactual. Third, the data from which the curvilinear forms were induced covered several settings, some of which showed primarily positive associations between satisfaction and desire, while others showed primarily negative correlations between satisfaction and desire. Fourth, both the satisfaction and the desire scales were summed from several items, rather than being based on single items; Dachler and Hulin (1969) acknowledged the likelihood that summed scales (such as the JDI) would be less likely to have artifactual properties than single items.

Generalization

The persons who provided data for the studies reported here were hardly a random sample of anything. We conducted research in the organizations that were willing to open their doors and with persons who were willing to participate. If an organization was willing, the participants generally were, too. The modal response rate across all of the systems was about 80 per cent.

Included in the studies were men and women of almost all ages from 14 to 65 and of all social classes. For the business organizations, it was possible to report separate analyses for employees and management because of the large sample sizes, but the other samples were smaller and did not lend themselves to such a breakdown. Even though the demographic range of the sample was wide, perhaps even comprehensive, there was some tendency for certain of the findings to be confounded with sample characteristics. Many, though by no means all, of the positive results pertaining to relatedness and growth needs were obtained from samples of predominantly younger men. The fraternities, Boys School, and Adolescent Lab generally had these qualities, although there were young women in Adolescent Lab. However, Adult Lab also provided findings relevant to relatedness and growth needs, and this population included men and women up through middle age and had no adolescents.

There was little reason to suspect that demographic factors were artifactually creating observed relationships, but our sampling procedure did not make it possible to systematically rule out or control for it, either.

The questions concerning methodology are complex and tedious ones, and the solutions we have offered are imperfect. In a number of different ways and at several different places, we have rested the case supporting various propositions on the convergence of findings from different settings, based on similar instruments tailored to fit the uniqueness of specific systems. Even though any given result might be discounted on methodological grounds, a series of findings which have different methodological problems may be explained away only by a series of methodological hypotheses whose total logic may be less parsimonious than the substantive hypotheses which the findings seem to support.

THEORETICAL IMPLICATIONS

So far, the major thrust in this work has been to test predictions made by E.R.G. theory against empirical data. However, there are also some general questions about theories that one might wish to ask. Whyte (1969) has provided one set of issues which will provide a starting point for evaluation. His list consisted of five characteristics of a useful theoretical framework. They were: parsimony, interrelatedness of concepts, objectifiability, measurability, and modifiability. To this list, along with Conant (1947) and Kuhn (1962), we add comparative utility, referring to how a given theory compares to other relevant theories on each of the five issues. In the case of E.R.G. theory, the most relevant comparisons are with Maslow's theory and the simple frustration hypothesis.

Parsimony

The criterion of parsimony asks whether one is using the fewest possible concepts to explain the phenomena of interest. Parsimony always must be balanced against comprehensiveness. A theory which employs more concepts but also explains more is not necessarily better or worse than a theory utilizing fewer concepts but also explaining less. One way to keep the criterion of parsimony manageable is to compare theories of similar scope, and in this way, the issue of comprehensiveness is held relatively constant. The problem addressed by all three views is how satisfaction relates to desire and vice versa.

The most parsimonious view is the simple frustration hypothesis which was well supported by much of the data collected in this series of studies. However, the data also showed how incomplete the hypothesis by itself was. It would not account for any of the relationships between broad need categories or for any of the positive relationships between satisfaction and desire. It would not predict the curvilinear relationships which were observed. Given these limitations, a more complex view of the problems was necessary. Maslow's theory and E.R.G. theory were major contenders.

In terms of need categories, E.R.G. theory is more parsimonious than Maslow's theory. It employs three major categories where Maslow used five. From the data obtained, it would appear that the three-category model was both more measureable (as shown by the factor analytic studies) and more predictive (as shown especially in the case of relatedness needs in Chapter 7).

E.R.G. theory is less parsimonious than Maslow's theory in the number of propositions it contains, but at the same time, it deals with more aspects of the satisfaction-desire problem than Maslow's theory. Maslow's theory deals only with upward movement through levels of hierarchy and implicitly with satisfaction and desire within each need category. E.R.G. theory deals with these problems and also with downward movement in the hierarchy and with the relationship between chronic desires and satisfaction. Overall, E.R.G. theory seems more comprehensive yet less parsimonious than Maslow's theory.

Another way that E.R.G. theory differs from Maslow's view is that it does not assume that lower-level gratification is necessary for higher-order needs to emerge. In none of the studies carried out in this series was the deprivation of existence needs very severe. Therefore, it was not possible to test this difference for the lowest-level needs. There were enough sufficiently unsatisfying interpersonal relationships in these samples to test the prepotency hypothesis from the interpersonal to the highest-order needs. In no case was there evidence indicating that the prepotency hypothesis was supported for this portion of the need hierarchy. Self-actualization or growth needs seemed to be present in our subjects regardless of their degree of interpersonal satisfaction.

Interrelatedness of Concepts

For the simple frustration hypothesis, the issue of interrelatedness of concepts is not relevant. Both Maslow's theory and E.R.G. theory have much to say about the interrelatedness of concepts. Neither theory is just a framework. However, it is also apparent by now that the amount of provision in the specification of relationships among concepts differs between the theories. Maslow's theory is less precise in the specification of relationships among concepts than E.R.G. theory. However, this is only a relative advantage of E.R.G. theory. Much more needs to be done with this theory in terms of increasing the precision with which the theory is stated. Ideally, this would eventually mean stating the theory by means of mathematical equations. It would also mean attempting to solve a series of differential equations for the equilibrium points implied by the deficiency and growth cycles.

Objectifiability and Measurability

Whyte proposed these criteria separately, but they are closely related, being roughly parallel to the reliability and validity of instruments based on the theory. By objectifiability, Whyte means the capacity of more than one investigator to agree upon how particular phenomena are to be described. Convergent validity (Campbell and Fiske, 1959) refers to finding high correlations between different measures of the same concept. Convergent validity has been shown for E.R.G. measures (Alderfer, 1967), but there was no known effort to use other than questionnaire measures for Maslow's concepts. By measurability, Whyte referred to the capacity to obtain some level of quantifiability of concepts. Concepts which have been validly quantified show reliability. Measures have been developed for both Maslow and E.R.G. concepts. The results of the factor analyses reported in Chapter 5 imply that the reliability of E.R.G. measures is greater than that of the Maslow measures.

Modifiability

Over the years, Maslow has been extraordinarily productive and prolific in his thinking and writing. He enriched and elaborated his ideas since "A Theory of Human Motivation" first appeared. However, this development has been carried on in such a way that one is not sure whether clearcut changes in the original formulation have been made. From reading a paper such as "Deficiency and Growth Motivation" (1955), one could conclude that the five-category system had been modified or dropped, but in still later work (Maslow, 1966) the original five categories reappear. Very little of this later work has been based on systematic data-collection procedures, although Maslow has readily cited the work of more systematically oriented investigators such as Carl Rogers. Perhaps it is fair to say that systematic data collection was not an important or central element in Maslow's style, while theoretical enrichment, elaboration, and expansion were.

The major mission of this whole book has been testing, elaborating, and modifying E.R.G. theory as a consequence of systematic empirical investigation.

Each of the preceding issues could be raised about any theory in any field. They do not pertain to a theory's substance. However, E.R.G. theory is concerned specifically with motivation. Lindzey (1958) developed a series of questions designed to underline the basic issues which tend to differentiate views about human motivation. These questions and the answers provided for E.R.G. theory are as follows:

1. *How important are conscious as opposed to unconscious motives in understanding human behavior?* E.R.G. theory does not utilize the conscious-vs.-unconscious construct, although there is nothing about any of the E.R.G. motives which implies that motives must be in awareness at all times. All the motives probably exist within and without awareness from time to time. Probably the

person most likely to have a high proportion of his needs out of his awareness is the one with chronically frustrated relatedness needs. This person in our society tends to be labeled neurotic or psychotic.

2. *What is the relative importance of direct as opposed to indirect techniques for assessing human motives?* Most of the data reported in this book have been based upon direct methods of measurement. At various times, I have experimented with ways to make it easier for people to report their subjective states to an investigator (Alderfer, 1968). It is a fine line between motives that are not revealed because the subject consciously chooses not to reveal them or because he unconsciously chooses not to reveal them. Therefore, the question about indirect measurement might be broadly conceived to include any method designed to enlarge the flow of socially unacceptable material. It is quite reasonable to think that projective techniques like the T.A.T. could be scored for E.R.G. needs.

3. *Is it essential, in assessing motives, to provide some appraisal of the ego processes, directive mechanisms, or cognitive controls that intervene between the motive and its expression?* E.R.G. theory is concerned with needs, not defenses or coping, but the measurement of satisfaction and desire is bound to improve if the respondent is not defending against expressing them.

4. *In assessing human motives, how important is it to specify the situational context within which the motives operate?* E.R.G. theory is not a theory about situations, but the necessity of considering situations for predictions about relatedness and growth needs has been readily underlined by the data indicating that propositions 2, 4, 6, and 7 seem to receive different degrees of support depending upon the degree of real satisfaction which seems possible in a particular setting.

5. *How necessary is knowledge about the past in the assessment of contemporary motivation?* The E.R.G. model, by taking account of individual differences in chronic needs, attempts both to provide a place for historically developed motives and to offer one kind of explanation for their development.

6. *At this time, is the area of motivation more in need of developing precise and highly objective measures of known motives or of identifying significant new motivational variables?* This question is more one of personal research style than something that could be answered theoretically. The present approach has been to attempt to maxi-

mize the constructive interaction between theoretical development and systematic empirical investigation. To improve investigation, better methods are needed. More precise data will most probably lead to refinements of theory.

7. *In attempting to understand human motivation is it advisable at present to focus upon one or a small number of motivational variables, or should an effort be made to appraise a wide array of variables? Do multivariate techniques of analysis have an indispensable contribution to offer to the study of human motivation?* By specifying three broad categories of human needs and also a means for defining specific needs within each category, E.R.G. theory attempts to partake of both worlds. Factor analysis was employed in the investigations reported here.

8. *What is the relative importance of detailed studies of individual cases, compared to carefully controlled experimental research and large-scale investigations?* This question also pertains more to personal style than to theoretical implications. All systematic methods have something to contribute to knowledge. This includes case studies, surveys, and laboratory studies. An important challenge facing anyone who would wish to obtain laboratory data relevant to testing E.R.G. theory would be how to create mutually satisfying interpersonal relationships in a social psychology laboratory. In this and other writers' opinion, this has not been done, but that does not rule out the possibility (Argyris, 1968; 1969).

9. *Is there a unique and important contribution to the understanding of human motives that can be made at present through the medium of comparative or lower-animal studies which cannot be duplicated by means of investigations utilizing human subjects?* The general answer to this question is yes. With specific regard to E.R.G. theory, the answer is more qualified. The theory is concerned with human motivation. While its development has been and will be continually stimulated by the results of animal studies, the theory could not be tested using animals as subjects.

NEW RESEARCH PROBLEMS

Two classes of new research problems arise in connection with the material presented here. The first concerns a number of ways in which E.R.G. theory could be tested in more exact and precise ways.

The second deals with how E.R.G. theory might be tied into other middle-range theories of individual motivation.

Empirical Research

The research reported in this volume consists of static and dynamic tests of E.R.G. theory in field settings. At a number of points in the treatment we have indicated some of the limitations of gathering data in this manner. Nevertheless, the combination of static and dynamic correlations was utilized for relatedness and growth needs but not for existence and relatedness needs. The choice in this matter was made in light of the author's interests and opportunities. But the fact remains that the propositions concerning existence needs and the relationship between existence and relatedness needs were not tested by dynamic correlations. Future field research could be fruitfully directed to obtaining longitudinal data on existence and relatedness needs where both are relatively unsatisfied.

During the current research, instruments were designed to fit the unique characteristics of particular settings. With the exception of the fraternity studies, in no two settings were exactly the same instruments employed. As a consequence, it was not possible to make direct comparisons between settings with respect to satisfaction levels except for the fraternities. It turned out to be very useful to make these kinds of comparisons between the fraternities. Now that instruments have been constructed for many different settings, however, it should be more feasible to construct a general E.R.G. satisfaction and desire questionnaire which would apply across settings with only minor changes to identify specific material objects, significant others, and environmental settings.

Perhaps the most challenging problem for future investigations is to conduct field and laboratory experiments to test E.R.G. propositions. The major rationale for carrying out the current series of studies in field settings was to be in touch with the phenomena in natural settings. If we really understand the phenomena of satisfaction and desire, it should be possible to begin reproducing them in laboratory settings in order to obtain more exact tests of causal direction. But, as many recent investigations have indicated, we are coming to understand that the social psychology laboratory is an organizational setting itself. Subjects sometimes try to please, outguess, or resist the experimenter (Rosenthal, 1966; Argyris, 1968). These conditions make the social psychology laboratory a setting whose culture needs to be changed if one is to be working with relatedness needs in a different condition than that of being relatively dissatisfied. Field experiments tend to contain fewer problems of this kind because to conduct a field experiment in these areas, it is usually necessary to establish a relationship of some mutuality with the subjects. At the same time, field experiments are not easy to arrange, nor do they typically provide the opportunities for experimental control which laboratory experiments do.

Theoretical Integration

Expectancy-instrumentality Theory Expectancy-instrumentality theory has received considerable support from systematic empirical research (Voorm, 1964; Galbraith and Cummings, 1967; Hackman and Porter, 1968; Porter and Lawler, 1968; Hunt and Hill, 1969). Some writers have tended to view "need theories," such as Maslow's, as being alternatives to expectancy-instrumentality theory (Hunt and Hill, 1969), while others (Campbell, Dunnette, Lawler, and Weick, 1970) are more likely to view the theories as complementary. Porter and Lawler (1968) in their version of expectancy-instrumentality theory provide a specific feedback loop from satisfaction to value of rewards. They suggest using Maslow's need categories as a way to distinguish which needs will increase in value as they are satisfied and which needs will decrease in value as they are satisfied. Whether the two types of theory are complementary depends on the problem one wishes to solve. Need theory alone does not attempt to predict performance or effort, while expectancy-instrumentality theory does predict to these dependent variables. Unless modified in the way suggested by Porter and Lawler (1968), expectancy-instrumentality theory does not predict motive strength. To predict effort or performance, an investigator using expectancy-instrumentality theory must make some assumptions about what people want or can get from exerting effort and performing effectively. In addition to Porter and Lawler's strategy of employing Maslow's theory, other investigators have used other strategies. Hackman and Porter (1968) used the inductive strategy of asking their subjects to give lists of positive and negative consequences of performing effectively.

Other investigators have used a strategy that parallels that of Porter and Lawler in that they have utilized lists of rewards that have a basis on one or more "need theories" (Graen, 1969; Galbraith and Cummings, 1967). A well-worked-out need theory would complement expectancy-instrumentality theory by defining rewards in terms of human needs.

Another way that need theory could aid expectancy-instrumentality theory is in spelling out the consequences of providing opportunities for various kinds of need satisfaction. This would be most useful when one wished to predict performance over time. Providing an incentive system which allowed a person to satisfy needs which diminished in desirability with increased satisfaction would contain the roots of destruction of the incentive system. However, providing an incentive system which allowed a person to satisfy needs which increased in desirability with increased satisfaction would strengthen the incentive system. The results of the present work also suggest that *not* knowing that some needs have a curvilinear relationship between satisfaction and desire could lead one mistakenly to conclude that an incentive system was not working, when in fact what happened was that a person had reached the minimum point of the satisfaction-desire curve and actually only needed more satisfaction opportunities in order for the particular relatedness or growth need to continue to be motivating. This kind of effect might be likely to happen in a job enlargement change where the new job was substantially more enriched than the old one but where it also approached the minimum point on the growth satisfaction-desire curve.

E.R.G. theory rests on the assumption that existence, relatedness, and growth needs are innate to human beings. Originally, these needs are not learned. However, this view does not rule out the possibility that the strength of the needs may also be increased as a result of learning as well as from satisfaction. From this perspective, instrumentality considerations may also play a part in determining the strength of a person's desires. A subordinate may learn, for example, that an open and trusting relationship with his boss is important if he is to satisfy his existence and growth needs. In this way, considerations from instrumentality-expectancy theory would also affect need theory as well as vice versa.

Two-factor Theory of Job Satisfaction Much of the controversy surrounding Herzberg's theory of job satisfaction has been on the issue of whether satisfaction and dissatisfaction are conceptually and operationally different (Dunnette, Campbell, and Hakel, 1967; Hinrichs and Mischkind, 1967). Herzberg's argument has been that the absence of hygiene factors contributes to dissatisfaction and the presence of motivators contributes to satisfaction. Among the motivators, Herzberg listed work itself, achievement, and responsibility. Among the hygiene factors, he listed interpersonal relations, salary, and working conditions. In a rough way, the factors called motivators are similar to growth needs, and those called hygiene factors are similar to relatedness and existence needs. There is one clear exception, however, which is recognition, a factor that Herzberg lists with the motivators. In E.R.G. terms, recognition would approximate a relatedness need.

Attempts to resolve the views of Herzberg and his critics have shown a tendency for both sides to discount the results of their opponents on the basis of methodological criticisms. In that way neither party is forced to take account of the other's data, which does not fit its own preconceptions. However, the curvilinear relationship between satisfaction and desire for both relatedness and growth needs provides some clues which may allow both Herzberg and his critics to have support for their views. Moreover, it does not require separating recognition from other interpersonal issues the way Herzberg does. Those critical of Herzberg have argued that most issues have both approach and avoidance properties and do not fit neatly into the hygiene-motivator dichotomy. The curvilinear relationships for relatedness and growth needs are consistent with this view but suggest that, for high levels of need satisfaction, increases in satisfaction may do more to increase approach tendencies, while for low levels of satisfaction, decreases in satisfaction may do more to increase avoidance tendencies. The findings regarding existence needs imply that material needs decrease with satisfaction and are therefore generally consistent with Herzberg's views.

PRACTICAL APPLICATIONS

The contribution of E.R.G. theory to organizational practice is indirect insofar as the practitioner's objective is to aid the achievement of organizational goals. Expectancy-instrumentality theory is much better designed for this purpose than E.R.G. theory. But E.R.G. theory offers other kinds of guidelines for effective action.

Diagnosing Motivational Problems

One practical value is the ability to diagnose motivational problems which are related to human needs. The theory proposed an exhaustive list of general human needs and mechanisms for defining specific cases of these needs. This itself can serve as a check list for anyone wishing systematically to think through the motivational issues involved in any action he might take.

It is not uncommon for organization members to realize that motivational problems which are not faced squarely result in side issues being discussed instead of the "real" concerns. E.R.G. theory provides a way to reason backwards from the concrete issue to more underlying concerns. One reaction a manager could have to a well-paid subordinate who asks for more money or space or better conditions is that this person will never be satisfied and therefore is ungrateful. Relying only on the concrete, manifest content of the subordinate's request, the manager might have a point. But suppose he went a step further and perhaps asked if there was any more to the question than the material request. Perhaps he could wonder if his own behavior toward the person might be giving messages that he was not aware of or did not intend. Another problem might arise when a manager noticed that an employee no longer seemed challenged in his job, seemed to resist change, and no longer expressed much interest in learning. One reaction to this phenomenon would be to decide that the man had run out of steam and was on the way to becoming a desk retiree. Another view would be to explore with the man whether he found his job challenging and whether together they might find ways to increase the degree to which he was fully utilized in his work. Another problem might be the high degree of solidarity among particular workers. It could be clear and open information that the employees restricted production and extensively initiated any new person joining the work group. One could credit this phenomenon to "blue collar attitudes" and dismiss it as beyond the control of management. It would also be possible to take the defensive group solidarity as a symptom rather than a disease and begin to see whether other unsatisfactory relationships with other groups or with a supervisor might be contributing to the problems.

Clarifying the Consequences of Managerial Styles

E.R.G. theory proposes that the kinds of satisfactions which are provided to a person determine the kind of rewards he will seek. If the theory is valid, then a manager may attempt to adjust his behavior and design his organization to foster either the existence deficiency cycle or the growth enrichment cycle. To keep the prime emphasis on existence needs would entail making sure that relatedness needs remained relatively dissatisfied. In practice, it would probably mean only that managers would choose to relate in traditional ways without work being given to develop relationships with mutuality in the exchange of feelings and ideas. The normal scarcity of most material factors when combined with dissatisfying interpersonal relations would probably serve to foster the existence deficiency cycle.

A manager wishing to aid the growth abundance cycle, on the other hand, would have to invest in developing unusually satisfying interpersonal relations and opportunities for people to utilize their capacities to a high degree. The results from the two business organizations studies here suggest that operating in the growth cycle is not common practice and may be very difficult to do. The results from the other organizations suggest that it is not impossible either.

The existence deficiency cycle and the growth abundance cycle have much in common with McGregor's (1960) concepts of theory X and theory Y managerial styles. The existence deficiency cycle forms the motivational basis for the set of assumptions in theory X management. The growth abundance cycle provides the motivational basis for the set of assumptions in theory Y management. Although interpersonal relations are not directly involved in either cycle, the state of relatedness satisfaction tends to foster one or the other pattern. Satisfying relationships tend to aid the growth cycle; dissatisfying relationships tend to support the deficiency cycle.

A Concluding Note

The main purpose of this work was to make a contribution toward understanding the relationship between need satisfaction and desire. The process of carrying out the investigation involved a continual dialogue between concepts and data and between theory and results. We started with a conceptual model and developed some instruments to test hypotheses derived from the model. Because the model was concerned with need satisfaction, we attempted to find diverse values of the various satisfactions. The search was undertaken in many different organizations, each of which made its own addition to the knowledge offered by the other settings. As a consequence of these investigations, the theory was elaborated and altered in some important ways. The case for E.R.G. theory now is based on correlational data from diverse field settings. The theory is not complete in all respects. More data and further conceptual refinements are needed. The revised version is offered as an improvement over existing models with the expectation that future work will result in additional modification and elaboration.

Appendix A

SAMPLE QUESTIONNAIRE FORMS

YALE UNIVERSITY
DEPARTMENT OF ADMINISTRATIVE SCIENCES
JOB ATTITUDE QUESTIONNAIRE

Nearly everyone has opinions about different features of his work. We would like to ask you how you feel about various parts of your job. All of the questions ask for your personal opinion. There are no right or wrong answers to any of the questions. Please answer the questions in the way that most accurately gives your opinion.

The questions were not designed to be tricky or difficult. In answering them, give the first response that occurs to you. Try not to spend a lot of time on any single question.

If there are comments that you would like to add, please do. Use the margins and blank spaces on the pages. All of your answers will be held in confidence. No one other than researchers at Yale University will ever see what you say.

The information provided in this study will be used for two purposes. The first is to provide a report of people's job attitudes for the organization's use. In this report, the results will be tabulated by groups. That way no individual will be identified, and the results can be useful. The second purpose is to add to what is known about how organizations operate. Along this line, the results might appear in a journal article or as part of a book. Here again, no person nor the organization will be identified.

In advance, we would like to thank you for participating in the study.

Sincerely,

Clayton Alderfer

CHRONIC DESIRE MEASURES

Ideal Job

1. Rank each of the following factors in the order of priority you give it to form the *ideal* job for you. Give a rank of "1" to the item that you **most** prefer in the ideal job, a rank of "8" to the item you **least** prefer, and so on for the factors in between.

2. After completing the ranking, then distribute 100 points among the eight factors: Give the highest number of points to the item you prefer **most,** the lowest number of points to the factor you prefer **least,** and so on for the items in between. After you have completed distributing the points, please check to be sure they add to 100.

Points	*Ranking*	
_____	_____	High salary
_____	_____	A chance to make full use of my abilities
_____	_____	Helpful and cooperative associates
_____	_____	Comprehensive fringe benefits
_____	_____	A boss who provides autonomy, help when needed, and recognition when deserved
_____	_____	Friendly, cordial relations with customers
_____	_____	Relative freedom from tension and pressure
_____	_____	Opportunities to learn new things

Total _____

SATISFACTION MEASURES

General Attitudes

Below are a number of statements dealing with your job experiences. Please indicate your degree of agreement or disagreement by writing the number 1, 2, 3, 4, 5, or 6 on the line just before the statement.

1. means *Strongly Agree*	4. means *Mildly Disagree*
2. means *Agree*	5. means *Disagree*
3. means *Mildly Agree*	6. means *Strongly Disagree*

Please Note: There are a number of questions about your "co-workers." When answering these, please think about the group of people with whom your job right now requires you to work most often and who are neither above nor below you in the organization.

_____ 1. I'm really a perfectionist about my work.

_____ 2. Our fringe benefits do not cover many of the areas they should.

_____ 3. I do things that I want to do.

_____ 4. I can count on my boss to do his job well.

_____ 5. I do things that make me feel safe when I am doing them.

_____ 6. I seldom get the feeling of learning new things from my work.

_____ 7. Compared to the rates for similar work here, my pay is good.

_____ 8. I do things where I can be creative.

_____ 9. My boss will play one person against another.

_____10. I have little confidence in top management.

_____11. I do things with people who are cooperative.

_____12. After work I still have a good deal of energy left for other things.

_____13. I do things that make me feel intelligent.

_____14. I have an opportunity to use many of my skills at work.

_____15. I find some customers extremely respectful of me.

_____16. Compared to similar jobs in other places, my pay is poor.

_____17. I do things with people who are friendly.

_____18. This organization is not a very good place to work.

_____19. I do things where I can find solutions to problems on my own.

_____20. The most important things that happen to me involve my work.

_____21. I do things I am dedicated to.

_____22. My coworkers are uncooperative unless it's to their advantage.

_____23. I do things which make me feel relaxed.

_____24. Top management can be counted on to do a good job.

_____25. I do things where others tell me how smart I am.

_____26. My job is very stressful.

_____27. I am unable to be very open with customers.

_____28. I do not make enough money from my job to live comfortably.

_____29. I do things where I can perform up to my abilities.

_____30. My boss takes account of my wishes and desires.

_____31. I do things where I can determine the way they are done.

_____32. The major satisfaction in my life comes from my work.

_____33. I do things which give me a feeling of prestige.

_____34. The fringe benefit program here gives nearly all the security I want.

_____35. I do things in which I have the opportunity to develop close friendships.

_____36. I can count on my coworkers to give me a hand when I need it.

_____37. I do things which I am content to do.

_____38. In my job I am often bored.

_____39. I find some customers rarely understand my point of view.

_____40. I have little confidence in my boss.

_____41. I do things that are easy for me.

_____42. I would probably not advise a person to choose a job like mine.

_____43. I do things which are helpful to others.

_____44. Compared to the rates for less demanding jobs, the pay for my job is poor.

_____45. I do things which give me a feeling of worthwhile accomplishment.

_____46. Most things in life are more important than work.

_____47. I do things where I can define the problem to be worked on.

_____48. My boss discourages people from making suggestions.

_____49. I do things that give me a feeling of self-esteem.

_____50. I often feel extremely tired at the end of a day.

_____51. I find that I am really able to be myself with customers.

_____52. I would probably advise a friend to apply for work here.

_____53. I do things where I can be independent.

_____54. I use a wide range of abilities in my work.

_____55. I do things that give me a feeling of self-fulfillment.

_____56. I cannot speak my mind to my coworkers.

_____57. I do things best when others are around.

_____58. My pay is adequate to provide for the basic things in life.

_____59. I do things that make me feel smart.

_____60. I am very much involved personally in my work.

_____61. I do things that are familiar.

_____62. It's easy to talk with my boss about my job.

_____63. I do things when others are around.

_____64. I feel completely safe from physical harm in the work that I do.

_____65. The fringe benefit program here needs improvement.

_____66. I do things where I can be imaginative.

_____67. My coworkers welcome opinions different from their own.

_____68. I do things in which I have a lot of opportunity for independent thought and action.

_____69. My job is a good one.

_____70. I do things that look like they will benefit me in the future.

_____71. My boss does not let me know when I could improve my performance.

_____72. I do things for which my accomplishments are recognized.

_____73. There is very little pressure associated with my job.

_____74. I do things that allow me to realize my potentialities.

_____75. I make one or more important decisions everyday.

_____76. I do things where I have a lot of authority.

_____77. My coworkers will not stick out their necks for me.

_____78. I do things that I feel I do better than anyone else.

_____79. My boss gives me credit when I do good work.

_____80. I do things where I am liked by others.

_____81. Compared to other places, our fringe benefits are excellent.

_____82. I do things which make me feel comfortable.

_____83. My boss expects people to do things his way.

_____84. I do not have the opportunity to do challenging things at work.

_____85. Considering the work required, the pay for my job is what it should be.

_____86. My boss keeps me informed about what is happening in the company.

_____87. I live, eat, and breathe my job.

_____88. I sense that my physical well-being is sometimes in danger in my work.

EPISODIC DESIRE MEASURES

Desires

Indicate how important and how much more you would like to attain in each of the following areas. Write the numbers 1, 2, 3, 4, or 5 on the lines after each item. Answer *both* importance and desired questions for each item.

1. means *Not Important*
2. means *Slightly Important*
3. means *Moderately Important*
4. means *Very Important*
5. means *Extremely Important*

1. means *No More*
2. means *Slightly More*
3. means *Somewhat More*
4. means *Much More*
5. means *Very Much More*

Cooperative relations with my coworkers
_____Importance
_____Desire

Developing new skills and knowledge at work
_____Importance
_____Desire

Good pay for my work
_____Importance
_____Desire

Respect from my boss
_____Importance
_____Desire

Feeling safe from physical danger

_____Importance

_____Desire

Frequent improvements in fringe benefits

_____Importance

_____Desire

Being accepted by others

_____Importance

_____Desire

Being challenged by my work

_____Importance

_____Desire

The feeling of prestige

_____Importance

_____Desire

Openness and honesty between my boss and me

_____Importance

_____Desire

Opportunity for independent thought and action

_____Importance

_____Desire

Respect from my coworkers

_____Importance

_____Desire

Feeling a sense of self-fulfillment

_____Importance

_____Desire

Making full use of my abilities at work

_____Importance

_____Desire

Friendly, cordial relations with customers

_____Importance

_____Desire

Frequent raises in pay

_____Importance

_____Desire

Having a sense of security
_____Importance
_____Desire

The opportunity to develop close friendships at work
_____Importance
_____Desire

Being liked by others
_____Importance
_____Desire

Mutual trust between my boss and me
_____Importance
_____Desire

A sense of self-esteem
_____Importance
_____Desire

A complete fringe benefit program
_____Importance
_____Desire

Thinking for myself
_____Importance
_____Desire

Openness and honesty with my coworkers
_____Importance
_____Desire

Opportunities for personal growth and development
_____Importance
_____Desire

Respect from customers
_____Importance
_____Desire

A sense of security from bodily harm
_____Importance
_____Desire

CORRELATION MATRICES

CORRELATION MATRIX FOR

(Bank Sample n = 217)

	2	3	4	5	6	7	8	9	10	11	12	13	14
1. Our fringe benefits do not cover many of the areas they should.	.03	−.18	.03	.06	−.16	.32	.05	−.12	.21	−.02	−.33	.00	.05
2. I seldom get the feeling of learning new things from my work.		−.13	.24	−.37	−.07	.19	.26	.31	.21	−.15	.09	−.24	.49
3. Compared to the rates for similar work here, my pay is good.			−.19	.30	.16	−.68	−.25	−.05	−.51	.09	.17	.13	−.06
4. My boss will play one person against another.				−.25	.02	.20	.35	.26	.16	−.45	−.13	−.26	.10
5. I have an opportunity to use many of my skills at work.					.11	−.26	−.26	−.16	−.36	.25	.12	.24	−.38
6. I find some customers extremely respectful of me.						−.26	.04	−.07	−.24	.07	.07	.08	−.16
7. Compared to similar jobs in other places, my pay is poor.							.23	.14	.57	−.15	−.19	−.15	.06
8. My coworkers are uncooperative unless it's to their advantage.								.28	.29	−.23	.07	−.47	−.23
9. I am unable to be very open with customers.									.16	−.09	.02	−.14	.12
10. I do not make enough money from my job to live comfortably.										−.19	−.21	−.29	.20
11. My boss takes account of my wishes and desires.											.25	.33	−.11
12. The fringe benefit program gives nearly all the security I want.												.06	. 02
13. I can count on my coworkers to give me a hand when I need it.													−.26
14. In my job I am often bored.													
15. I find some customers rarely understand my point of view.													
16. Compared to the rates for less demanding jobs, the pay for my job is poor.													
17. My boss discourages people from making suggestions.													
18. I find that I am really able to be myself with customers.													
19. I use a wide range of abilities in my work.													
20. I cannot speak my mind to my coworkers.													
21. My pay is adequate to provide for the basic things in life.													
22. It's easy to talk with my boss about my job.													
23. I feel completely safe from physical harm in the work I do.													
24. The fringe benefit program here needs improvement.													
25. My coworkers welcome opinions different from their own.													
26. My boss does not let me know when I could improve my performance.													
27. I make one or more important decisions everyday.													
28. My coworkers will not stick out their necks for me.													
29. My boss gives me credit when I do good work.													
30. Compared to other places, our fringe benefits are excellent.													
31. My boss expects people to do things his way.													
32. I do not have an opportunity to do challenging things at work.													
33. Considering the work required, the pay for my job is what it should be.													
34. My boss keeps me informed about what is happening in the company.													
35. I sense that my physical well-being is sometimes in danger in my work.													

E.R.G. SATISFACTION ITEMS

15	*16*	*17*	*18*	*19*	*20*	*21*	*22*	*23*	*24*	*25*	*26*	*27*	*28*	*29*	*30*	*31*	*32*	*33*	*34*	*35*
.16	.21	.13	.06	.05	.07	-.11	-.04	-.11	.58	.02	.10	-.08	.02	-.06	-.51	.11	-.02	-.13	-.13.	.05
.19	.23	.20	-.07	-.35	-.05	-.09	-.17	-.13	-.05	-.25	.13	-.29	.15	-.25	-.05	.11	.46	-.03	-.20	.15
-.07	-.63	-.14	.05	.25	-.21	.48	.13	-.06	-.11	.18	-.03	.09	-.17	.21	.23	-.14	-.21	.64	.20	-.03
.33	.19	.44	-.01	-.14	.27	-.21	-.50	-.19	.00	-.22	.25	-.08	.20	-.40	-.11	.21	.23	-.16	-.29	.23
-.16	-.21	-.18	.15	.60	-.10	.18	.29	.06	-.04	.20	-.06	.29	-.17	.30	.09	-.17	-.48	.19	.29	-.01
-.21	-.22	-.19	.27	.08	.03	.20	.11	-.06	-.06	.00	-.19	.22	.09	.18	.11	-.05	-.04	.12	-.03	.10
.17	.65	.20	-.10	-.13	.18	-.45	-.16	-.04	.24	-.11	.15	-.16	.19	-.26	-.30	.15	.21	-.55	-.28	.00
.21	.30	.36	.05	-.16	.39	-.21	-.36	-.11	.02	-.39	.14	-.12	.46	-.40	-.11	-.20	.38	-.22	-.34	.22
.37	.13	.12	-.32	-.09	.08	-.16	-.19	-.02	.02	-.08	.07	-.13	.21	-.16	-.06	.16	.25	-.05	-.18	.91
.13	.52	.30	-.10	-.27	.22	-.46	-.24	-.08	.13	-.22	.10	-.22	.33	-.29	-.31	.19	.33	-.45	-.28	.06
-.16	-.18	-.53	.02	.11	-.26	.16	.57	.13	-.11	.23	-.35	.07	-.36	.54	.13	-.23	-.27	.20	.37	-.11
-.15	-.16	-.19	.04	.05	-.03	.18	.20	.23	-.52	-.03	-.11	-.02	-.03	.12	.50	-.04	-.01	.26	.09	-.06
-.13	-.17	-.22	.07	.15	-.18	.29	.34	.23	-.06	.44	-.20	.15	-.34	.36	.21	-.12	-.26	.21	.30	-.12
.32	.13	.14	-.19	-.42	.07	-.07	-.21	-.10	-.03	-.22	.09	-.26	.25	-.13	.00	.12	.50	.02	-.08	.02
	.21	.23	-.22	-.03	.10	-.13	-.21	-.13	.19	-.09	.26	-.10	.25	-.13	-.15	.15	.25	-.10	-.19	.19
		.24	-.10	-.17	.20	-.49	-.24	-.11	.20	-.21	.21	-.06	.26	-.31	-.26	.19	.29	-.60	-.30	.09
			-.06	-.10	.31	-.17	-.61	-.07	.18	-.18	.36	-.01	.28	-.46	-.13	.30	.37	-.17	-.33	.16
				.04	-.05	.10	.15	-.04	-.05	.02	-.14	.06	-.05	-.01	.01	.03	-.08	.08	-.03	.05
				-.12	.18	.24	.02	.18	.29	.03	.46	-.13	.16	.00	-.07	-.47	.11	.17	-.01	
				-.16	-.29	-.11	-.02	-.42	.07	.00	.38	-.22	-.03	.15	.32	-.13	-.25	.20		
							.17	.11	-.10	.25	-.12	.13	-.20	.19	.20	-.09	-.25	.47	.20	-.01
							.11	-.09	.20	-.42	.08	-.29	.59	.22	-.23	-.37	.15	.41	-.20	
									-.08	.13	.01	.02	-.11	.08	.13	-.02	.02	.11	.03	-.51
										.15	.25	.13	.03	-.11	-.61	.06	-.06	-.19	-.09	.06
											-.09	.17	-.41	.30	-.04	.30	-.28	.14	.28	-.11
												.05	.23	-.40	-.22	.15	.24	-.07	-.31	.15
													.03	.02	.19	.07	-.28	-.02	.10	.07
														-.19	.00	.39	.42	-.18	-.29	.20
														.16	-.25	-.24	.24	.48	-.10	
															-.01	-.07	.30	.20	-.01	
															.26	-.09	-.20	.14		
																	-.13	-.38	.18	
																		.25	.01	
																			-.12	

Appendix C

CORRELATION MATRIX FOR

(Bank Sample n=217)

	2	3	4	5	6	7	8	9	10	11	12	13
1. Cooperative relations with my coworkers —Important.	.02	.37	.06	.27	.02	.33	-.09	.20	-.12	.17	-.02	.08
2. Cooperative relations with my coworkers —More.		-.08	.28	-.03	.35	-.14	.60	.09	.38	.00	.20	.03
3. Developing new skills and knowledge at work—Important.			.43	.40	.14	.38	-.02	.17	-.03	.23	.07	.41
4. Developing new skills and knowledge at work—More.				.09	.27	.10	.24	.13	.15	.16	.27	.31
5. Good pay for my work—Important.					.34	.34	.07	.22	.04	.34	.24	.16
6. Good pay for my work—More.						-.10	.41	.12	.16	.19	.28	.05
7. Respect from my boss—Important.							.03	.27	.01	.27	.10	.29
8. Respect from my boss—More.								.12	.42	.16	.29	.11
9. Feeling safe from physical danger— —Important.									.41	.43	.17	.05
10. Feeling safe from physical danger— More.										.31	.46	.03
11. Frequent improvements in fringe benefits—Important.											.54	.11
12. Frequent improvements in fringe benefits—More.												.12
13. Being challenged by my work— Important.												
14. Being challenged by my work—More.												
15. Openness and honesty between my boss and me—Important.												
16. Openness and honesty between my boss and me—More.												
17. Respect from my coworkers—Important.												
18. Respect from my coworkers—More.												
19. Making full use of my abilities— Important.												
20. Making full use of my abilities—More.												
21. Friendly, cordial relations with customers—Important.												
22. Friendly, cordial relations with customers—More.												
23. Frequent raises in pay—Important.												
24. Frequent raises in pay—More.												
25. Mutual trust between my boss and me— Important.												
26. Mutual trust between my boss and me— More.												
27. A complete fringe benefit program— Important.												
28. A complete fringe benefit program— More.												
29. Openness and honesty with my coworkers —Important.												
30. Openness and honesty with my coworkers —More.												
31. Respect from customers—Important.												
32. Respect from customers—More.												
33. A sense of security from bodily harm— Important.												
34. A sense of security from bodily harm— More.												

E.R.G. DESIRE ITEMS

14	15	16	17	18	19	20	21	22	23	24	25	26	27	28	29	30	31	32	33	34
-.14	.44	-.02	.28	-.05	.29	.02	.17	-.09	.13	-.02	.34	-.01	.23	-.03	.34	-.03	.15	-.12	.23	.00
.38	.01	.61	.01	.55	.01	.35	.08	.46	.04	.20	-.06	.58	.05	.26	.02	.59	.07	.49	.07	.31
.05	.28	.01	.37	-.06	.42	.14	.17	.01	.19	.06	.18	.02	.26	.11	.34	.02	.17	.03	.16	.05
.30	.11	.21	.17	.13	.24	.36	.11	.18	.11	.09	.08	.24	.14	.22	.21	.18	.13	.23	.11	.15
-.01	.13	.02	.26	-.02	.20	.10	.09	-.03	.51	.29	.10	.00	.35	.23	.18	.01	.08	.07	.17	.10
.24	-.01	.36	.03	.30	-.01	.32	-.15	.24	.33	.67	-.09	.36	.21	.35	.10	.30	-.05	.36	.08	.25
-.11	.42	-.15	.50	-.09	.43	.01	.42	.03	.13	-.10	.46	-.13	.24	.06	.37	-.10	.37	.05	.26	.05
.43	.02	.69	.03	.56	.01	.39	.00	.50	.08	.31	-.06	.64	.07	.37	.04	.53	.02	.52	.05	.40
-.01	.12	.09	.23	.09	.18	.04	.34	.17	.34	.21	.13	.09	.28	.18	.27	.10	.26	.16	-.18	.37
.28	-.02	.42	.12	.44	.04	.21	.16	.52	.19	.26	-.01	.43	.11	.49	.11	.46	.19	.49	.36	.80
-.02	.15	.04	.30	.12	.19	.17	.09	.13	.41	.30	.14	.12	.44	.46	.24	.10	.21	.10	.45	.34
.23	.10	.21	.12	.31	.08	.28	-.01	.34	.23	.33	.05	.32	.20	.72	.12	.33	.17	.35	.16	.43
.40	.26	.02	.30	-.01	.55	.15	.24	-.01	.09	.05	.33	.07	.17	-.02	.36	-.01	.17	.10	-.02	.07
	.01	.42	.00	.37	.19	.56	-.06	.33	-.09	.24	-.02	.37	.03	.19	-.02	.36	-.10	.34	-.12	.24
		.01	.31	-.07	.36	.07	.21	-.13	.18	-.04	.67	-.01	.23	.02	.46	-.10	.24	-.09	.18	.04
			-.01	.59	-.08	.42	-.02	.51	.08	.36	-.07	.78	.04	.36	.00	.60	.05	.55	.08	.47
				.11	.48	.08	.35	.10	.27	.02	.40	.05	.34	.15	.54	.03	.39	.10	.27	.20
					-.06	.42	-.05	.61	.07	.36	-.17	.63	.00	.41	.01	.73	-.01	.58	.06	.48
						.25	.35	.04	.17	-.04	.38	.02	.42	.14	.48	-.02	.21	.04	.21	.10
							.00	.40	.10	.34	-.02	.43	.11	.32	.00	.39	-.02	.40	.01	.23
								.25	.15	-.12	.37	.00	.34	.03	.36	.01	.65	.16	.32	.16
									.09	.33	-.09	.58	.05	.49	.00	.13	.21	.79	.10	.49
										.51	.24	.10	.34	.26	.30	.08	.21	.16	.32	.16
											-.07	.38	.17	.41	.02	.33	-.02	.43	.18	.36
												.00	.29	-.02	.51	-.14	-.35	-.03	.21	.13
													.05	.48	.02	.67	.14	.65	.06	.49
														.35	.43	.03	.34	.12	.34	.17
															.12	.50	.18	.51	.16	.52
																.04	.32	.04	.27	.15
																	.04	.62	.04	.49
																		.31	.34	.21
																			.12	. 53
																				.44

CORRELATION MATRIX FOR THE

(Bank Sample n=217)

	2	3	4	5	6	7	8	9	10	11	12	13	14
1. I do things I want to do.	.03	.22	.29	.06	.16	.28	.21	.21	.22	.23	.23	.19	.15
2. I do things that make me feel safe when I am doing them.		−.06	.16	.28	.23	.08	.10	.40	.15	.11	.20	.07	.17
3. I do things where I can be creative.			.17	.34	.17	.21	.26	−.02	.09	.39	.21	.29	.20
4. I do things with people who are cooperative.				.26	.58	.23	.13	.30	.14	.16	.19	.20	.22
5. I do things that make me feel intelligent.					.18	.21	.35	.28	.27	.46	.41	.42	.25
6. I do things with people who are friendly.						.15	.12	.26	.14	−.02	.12	.18	.19
7. I do things where I can find solutions to problems on my own.							.20	.09	.17	.26	.27	.20	.12
8. I do things I am dedicated to.								.24	.20	.32	.23	.29	.31
9. I do things which make me feel relaxed.									.24	.15	.18	.33	.28
10. I do things where others tell me how smart I am.										.15	.17	.39	.16
11. I do things where I can perform up to my abilities.											.38	.43	.22
12. I do things where I can determine the way they are done.												.32	.22
13. I do things which give me a feeling of prestige.													.32

14. I do things in which I have the opportunity to develop close friendships.
15. I do things which I am content to do.
16. I do things that are easy for me.
17. I do things which are helpful to others.
18. I do things which give me the feeling of worthwhile accomplishment.
19. I do things where I can define the problem to be worked on.
20. I do things that give me a feeling of self esteem.
21. I do things where I can be independent.
22. I do things that give me a feeling of self-fulfillment.
23. I do things best when others are around.
24. I do things that make me feel smart.
25. I do things that are familiar.
26. I do things when others are around.
27. I do things where I can be imaginative.
28. I do things in which I have a lot of opportunity for independent thought and action.
29. I do things that look like they will benefit me in the future.
30. I do things for which my accomplishments are recognized.
31. I do things that allow me to realize my potentialities.
32. I do things where I have a lot of authority.
33. I do things that I feel I do better than anyone else.
34. I do things where I am liked by others.
35. I do things which make me feel comfortable.

MASLOW SATISFACTION ITEMS

15	16	17	18	19	20	21	22	23	'24	25	26	27	28	29	30	31	32	33	34	35
.19	.18	.07	.13	.16	.14	.16	.08	.04	.24	.31	.17	.19	.20	.22	.24	.21	.21	.17	.14	.22
.30	-.01	.08	-.02	.05	.13	.06	.05	-.05	.24	.21	.02	-.19	-.06	.18	.09	.09	-.18	-.04	.22	.47
.15	-.19	.18	.41	.15	.25	.24	.47	.02	.29	-.15	-.10	.65	.46	.26	.29	.47	.28	.11	.05	.10
.32	-.10	.05	.20	.18	.25	.20	.17	.08	.24	.17	.09	.10	.17	.27	.14	.15	.00	-.05	.20	.32
.38	-.15	.34	.55	.29	.50	.28	.49	.02	.50	.07	.09	.25	.32	.33	.33	.37	.20	.06	.28	.47
.27	-.01	.02	.14	.05	.19	.14	.12	.03	.24	.17	.05	.06	.11	.16	.12	.18	-.10	-.01	.32	.37
.14	-.02	.19	.21	.20	.14	.29	.20	-.01	.26	.06	.18	.24	.24	.18	.20	.18	.17	.14	.14	.15
.24	-.22	.37	.45	.22	.33	.13	.38	.08	.23	-.07	.04	.23	.30	.27	.24	.42	.19	.05	.12	.21
.31	.11	.11	.15	.13	.35	.18	.14	.02	.36	.28	.09	-.10	.01	.30	.08	.12	-.06	.07	.35	.56
.22	.10	.15	.14	.08	.21	.13	.19	.11	.44	.19	.19	.12	.16	.13	.19	.18	.17	.24	.15	.31
.29	-.26	.30	.61	.26	.31	.25	.58	.07	.33	-.01	.03	.41	.33	.39	.27	.54	.31	.01	-.03	.18
.27	-.05	.38	.38	.36	.40	.34	.36	.03	.32	.18	.12	.25	.37	.26	.23	.30	.19	.05	.08	.24
.31	.01	.19	.43	.28	.57	.20	.46	.21	.57	.10	.04	.37	.25	.33	.32	.45	.36	.24	.21	.38
.33	.00	.17	.18	.17	.24	.13	.20	.23	.32	.14	.09	.20	.16	.23	.13	.26	.18	.04	.24	.44
	.09	.22	.31	.20	.35	.22	.32	.07	.38	.27	.04	.14	.18	.21	.32	-.05	.19	.15	.06	
		-.11	-.24	.03	-.01	-.02	-.22	.06	.10	.34	.28	-.15	-.18	-.20	-.07	-.18	.18	-.05	-.03	.21
			.34	.14	.20	.18	.29	.01	.08	.00	.10	.16	.29	.18	.12	.24	.35	.09	.12	.24
				.35	.47	.34	.72	.00	.38	-.06	.00	.46	.44	.41	.32	.59	.19	.10	.14	.22
					.39	.17	.27	.11	.16	.12	.12	.22	.32	.22	.35	.19	.20	.18	.29	.45
						.24	.52	.15	.59	.10	.15	.33	.36	.34	.29	.37	.21	.12	.14	.21
							.30	.02	.30	.08	.16	.32	.40	.16	.04	.21	.35	.04	.10	.20
								.06	.42	-.16	-.04	.53	.49	.40	.28	.62	.08	.11	.12	.12
									.24	-.01	.31	.12	.06	.07	.13	.09	.08	.11	.12	.12
										.25	.26	.28	.23	.28	.30	.43	.20	.32	.44	.46
											.32	-.18	-.08	.07	.02	-.08	-.04	.13	.35	.41
												-.03	.11	.04	.10	.02	.00	.17	.20	.20
													.56	.34	.35	.52	.49	.20	-.02	.05
														.41	.27	.44	.40	.09	.07	.13
															.30	.38	.27	.02	.16	.30
																.44	.30	.11	.21	.22
																	.34	.17	.10	.15
																		.24	.01	-.03
																			.12	.10
																				.42

Appendix E

CORRELATION MATRIX FOR THE MASLOW DESIRE ITEMS

(Bank Sample n=217)

	2	3	4	5	6	7	8	9	10	11	12	13	14	15	16	17	18	19	20
1. Being accepted by others—Important.	.23	.39	.17	.30	.06	.36	.08	.41	.17	.46	.24	.64	.24	.29	.11	.14	-.04	.27	-.01
2. Being accepted by others—More.		.22	.47	.10	.45	.07	.49	.22	.56	.27	.57	.32	.61	.19	.50	.07	.40	.13	.35
3. The feeling of prestige—Important.			.65	.24	.23	.34	.22	.24	.26	.36	.20	.43	.25	.43	.36	.21	.15	.26	.15
4. The feeling of prestige—More.				.15	.42	.18	.46	.22	.48	.23	.36	.32	.39	.33	.56	.05	.35	.15	.39
5. Opportunity for independent thought and action—Important.					.21	.38	.12	.13	.06	.04	.06	.15	.10	.39	.18	.40	.12	.47	.24
6. Opportunity for independent thought and action—More.						.10	.54	.22	.52	.23	.47	.17	.43	.21	.50	.16	.60	.24	.47
7. Feeling a sense of self-fulfillment—Important.							.30	.21	.02	.21	.07	.24	.04	.39	.21	.36	.09	.48	.17
8. Feeling a sense of self-fulfillment—More.								.08	.49	.12	.37	.15	.39	.19	.47	.13	.47	.20	.46
9. Having a sense of security—Important.									.42	.34	.24	.43	.21	.28	.57	.05	-.01	.30	.11
10. Having a sense of security—More.										.31	.59	.27	.60	.15	.25	.05	.49	.08	.35
11. The opportunity to develop close friendships at work—Important.											.60	.57	.29	.28	.18	.16	.07	.19	.00
12. The opportunity to develop close friendships at work—More.												.31	.62	.22	.57	.05	.42	.08	.30
13. Being liked by others—Important.													.39	.34	.20	.17	.05	.33	.15
14. Being liked by others—More.														.19	.59	.03	.46	.16	.39
15. A sense of self esteem—Important.															.40	.26	.13	.41	.25
16. A sense of self esteem—More.																.14	.59	.23	.56
17. Thinking for myself—Important.																	.18	.48	.13
18. Thinking for myself—More.																		.11	.51
19. Opportunities for personal growth and development—Important.																			.46
20. Opportunities for personal growth and development—More.																			

BIBLIOGRAPHY

Ainsworth, M. S.: Further Research into the Adverse Effects of Maternal Deprivation. In Bowlby, J.: *Child Care and the Growth of Love*, 2nd ed. Baltimore, Penguin, 1965, pp. 191–241.

Alderfer, C. P.: Comparison of Questionnaire Responses with and without Preceding Interviews. *J. of Applied Psychology*, 1968, 52, 335–340.

Alderfer, C. P.: Convergent and Discriminant Validation of Satisfaction and Desire Measures by Interviews and Questionnaires. *J. of Applied Psychology*, 1967, 51, 509–520.

Alderfer, C. P.: An Empirical Test of a New Theory of Human Needs. *Organizational Behavior and Human Performance*, 1969, 4, 142–175.

Alderfer, C. P. and L. D. Brown: The Human System of Boys School. Mimeograph, Department of Administrative Sciences, Yale University, 1970.

Alderfer, C. P. and T. M. Lodahl: A Study of Climate and Culture in College Fraternities, under review, 1970.

Alderfer, C. P. and C. G. McCord. Personal and Situational Factors in the Recruitment Interview, *J. of Applied Psychology*, 1970, 54, 377–385.

Allport, G. W.: *Becoming*. New Haven, Yale University Press, 1955.

Allport, G. W.: The Open System in Personality Theory. *J. of Abnormal and Social Psychology*, 1960, 61, 301–311.

Allport, G. W.: *Pattern and Growth in Personality*. New York, Holt, Rinehart, and Winston, 1961.

Andrews, F. M.: The Scientist and his Administrative Chief. Analysis memo, Survey Research Center, University of Michigan, 1962.

Argyris, C.: The Incompleteness of Social Psychological Theory. *American Psychologist*, 1969, 24, 893–908.

Argyris, C.: *Integrating the Individual and the Organization*. New York, John Wiley, 1964.

Argyris, C.: *Interpersonal Competence and Organizational Effectiveness*. Homewood, Ill., Dorsey Press, 1962.

Ash, P.: The S.R.A. Inventory: A Statistical Analysis. *Personnel Psychology*, 1954, 7, 337–364.

Atkinson, J. W.: *Motives in Fantasy, Action, and Society*. New York, Van Nostrand, 1958.

Baehr, M. E.: A Factorial Study of the S.R.A. Employee Inventory. *Personnel Psychology*, 1954, 7, 319–336.

Barker, R. G.: *Ecological Psychology*. Stanford, Stanford University Press, 1968.

Barker, R. G., T. Dembo, and K. Lewin. Frustration and Regression. In R. G. Barker, *et al.* (Eds.): *Child Behavior and Development*. New York, McGraw-Hill, 1943, pp. 441–458.

Barnes, L. B.: *Organizational Systems and Engineering Groups*. Boston, Harvard Graduate School of Business, 1960.

Baumgartel, H.: Leadership Style as a Variable in Research Administration. *Administrative Science Quarterly*, 1957, 2, 344–360.

Beer, M.: *Leadership, Employee Needs, and Motivation*. Columbus, Ohio, Bureau of Business Research, Ohio State University, 1966.

Berkowitz, L.: *The Development of Motives and Values in the Child*. New York, Basic Books, 1964.

Berkowitz, L.: Social Motivation. In Lindzey, G. and E. Aronson (Eds.): *Handbook of Social Psychology*, 2nd ed., vol. III. Reading, Mass., Addison-Wesley, 1969, pp. 50–135.

von Bertalenffy, L.: *General System Theory*. New York, George Braziller, 1968.

Bettelheim, B.: *The Children of the Dream*. New York, Macmillan, 1969.

Blalock, H. M.: *Social Statistics*. New York, McGraw-Hill, 1960.

Bowlby, J.: *Child Care and the Growth of Love*, 2nd ed. Baltimore, Penguin, 1965.

Bradford, L., J. Gibb, and K. Benne: *T-group Theory and Laboratory Method*. New York, Wiley, 1964.

Bunker, D. R.: Individual Applications of Laboratory Training. *J. of Applied Behavioral Science*, 1965, 1, 131–148.

Campbell, D. T. and D. W. Fiske: Convergent and Discriminant Validation by the Multitrait-multimethod Matrix. *Psychological Bulletin*, 1959, 56, 81–105.

Campbell, J. P., M. D. Dunnette, E. E. Lawler, and K. E. Weick: *Managerial Behavior, Performance, and Effectiveness*. New York, McGraw-Hill, 1970.

Clark, J. B.: Motivation in Work Groups: A Tentative View. *Human Organization*, 1960–61, 13, 198–208.

Cofer, C. N. and M. H. Appley: *Motivation: Theory and Research*. New York, John Wiley, 1964.

Cohen, A. K.: *Deviance and Social Control*. Englewood Cliffs, N.J., Prentice-Hall, 1966.

Cohen, J.: *Secondary Motivation: I, Personal Motives*. Chicago, Rand McNally, 1970.

Conant, J. B.: *On Understanding Science*. New Haven, Yale University Press, 1947.

Cronbach, L. J.: The Two Disciplines of Scientific Psychology. *American Psychologist*, 1957, 12, 671–684.

Dabas, Z. S.: The Dimensions of Morale: An Item Factorization of the S.R.A. Employee Inventory. *Personnel Psychology*, 1958, 11, 217–234.

Dachler, H. P. and C. L. Hulin: A Reconsideration of the Relationship between Satisfaction and Judged Importance of Environmental and Job Characteristics. *Organizational Behavior and Human Performance*, 1969, 4, 252–266.

Drevdahl, J. E.: Some Developmental and Environmental Factors in Creativity. In Taylor, C. (Ed.): *Widening Horizons in Creativity*. New York, John Wiley, 1964, pp. 170–186.

Dunnette, M. D.: The Motives of Industrial Managers. *Organizational Behavior and Human Performance*, 1967, 2, 176–181.

Dunnette, M. D.: *Personnel Selection and Placement.* Belmont, Calif., Wadsworth, 1966.

Dunnette, M. D., J. D. Campbell, and M. D. Hakel: Factors Contributing to Job Satisfaction and Job Dissatisfaction in Six Occupational Groups. *Organizational Behavior and Human Performance*, 1967, 2, 143–174.

Etzioni, A.: Basic Human Needs, Alienation and Inauthenticity. *American Sociological Review*, 1968, 33, 870–885.

Fiske, D. W. and S. R. Maddi (Eds.): *Functions of Varied Experience.* Homewood, Ill., Dorsey, 1961.

Franklin, J. C., B. C. Schiele, J. Brozek, and A. Keys: Observations on Human Behavior in Experimental Semistarvation and Rehabilitation. *Journal of Clinical Psychology*, 1948, 4, 28–45.

Freud, S.: *Therapy and Technique.* New York, Collier, 1963.

Friedmann, G.: *The Anatomy of Work.* Glencoe, Free Press, 1961.

Fromm, E.: *The Art of Loving.* New York, Holt, Rinehart, and Winston, 1956.

Fromm, E.: *Man for Himself.* New York, Holt, Rinehart, and Winston, 1947.

Galbraith, J. and L. L. Cummings: An Empirical Investigation of the Motivational Determinants of Task Performance: Interactive Effects between Instrumentality-valence and Motivation-ability. *Organizational Behavior and Human Performance*, 1967, 2, 237–257.

Gewirtz, J. L. and D. M. Baer: Deprivation and Satiation of Social Reinforcers as Drive Conditions. *J. of Abnormal and Social Psychology*, 1958a, 57, 165–172.

Gewirtz, J. L. and D. M. Baer: The Effect of Brief Social Deprivation on Behaviors for a Social Reinforcer. *J. of Abnormal and Social Psychology*, 1958b, 56, 49–56.

Gompers, S.: *Labor and the Common Welfare.* New York, Dutton, 1919.

Goodman, R. A.: On the Operationality of the Maslow Need Hierarchy. *British Journal of Industrial Relations*, 1968, 6, 51–57.

Gordon, O. J.: A Factor Analysis of Human Needs and Industrial Morale. *Personnel Psychology*, 1955, 8, 1–18.

Graen, G.: Instrumentality Theory of Work Motivation. *J. of Applied Psychology Monograph*, 1969, 53, 1–25.

Hackman, J. R. and E. E. Lawler: Job Characteristics and Employee Motivation: An Empirical Investigation. *J. of Applied Psychology*, 1971, in press.

Hackman, J. R. and L. W. Porter: Expectancy Theory Predictions of Work Effectiveness. *Organizational Behavior and Human Performance*, 1968, 3, 417–426.

Haire, M., E. Ghiselli, and L. W. Porter: *Managerial Thinking.* New York, John Wiley, 1966.

Hall, D. T. and K. E. Nougaim: An Examination of Maslow's Need Hierarchy in an Organizational Setting. *Organizational Behavior and Human Performance*, 1968, 3, 12–35.

Hall, J. F.: *The Psychology of Motivation.* New York, Lippincott, 1961.

Harlow, H. F.: Love in Infant Monkeys. *Scientific American*, 1959, 200, 68–74.

Harlow, H. F.: Mice, Monkeys, Men, and Motives. *Psychological Review*, 1953, 60, 23–32.

Harlow, H. F. and M. K. Harlow: Social Deprivation in Monkeys. *Scientific American*, 1962, 207, 136–146.

Harrison, R.: A Conceptual Framework for Laboratory Training. Mimeo, 1966.

Harrison, R.: Cumulative Communality Cluster Analysis of Workers' Job Attitudes. *J. of Applied Psychology,* 1961, 45, 123–125.

Harrison, R.: Impact of the Laboratory on Perceptions of Others by Experimental Group. In Argyris, C.: *Interpersonal Competence and Organizational Effectiveness.* Homewood, Ill., Dorsey, 1962, pp. 261–285.

Harrison, R.: Sources of Variation in Managers' Job Attitudes. *Personnel Psychology,* 1960, 13, 425–434.

Harvey, O. J., D. E. Hunt, and H. M. Schroder: *Conceptual Systems and Personality Organization,* New York, Wiley, 1961.

Heron, W., B. K. Doane, and T. H. Scott: Visual Disturbances after Prolonged Perceptual Isolation. *Canadian J. of Psychology,* 1956, 10, 13–18.

Hill, K. T. and H. W. Stevenson: Effect of Social Reinforcement Following Social and Sensory Deprivation. *J. of Abnormal and Social Psychology,* 1964, 68, 579–584.

Hinrichs, J. R.: A Replicated Study of Job Satisfaction Dimensions. *Personnel Psychology,* 1968, 21, 479–503.

Hinrichs, J .R. and L. A. Mischkind: Empirical and Theoretical Limitations of the Two-factor Hypothesis of Job Satisfaction. *J. of Applied Psychology,* 1967, 51, 191–200.

Holmberg, A. R.: *Nomads of the Long Bow: The Siriano of Eastern Bolivia.* Chicago, University of Chicago Press, 1960.

Homans, G. C.: *Social Behavior: Its Elementary Forms.* New York, Harcourt, Brace, and World, 1961.

Horney, K. *The Neurotic Personality of our Time.* New York, Norton, 1937.

Horney, K. *Our Inner Conflicts.* New York, Norton, 1945.

Hunt, J. G. and J. W. Hill: The New Look in Motivation Theory for Organization Research. *Human Organization,* 1969, 28, 100–109.

Jacques, E.: *Equitable Payment.* New York, Wiley, 1961.

Jezernik, M. D.: Changes in the Hierarchy of Motivational Factors and Social Values in Slovenian Industry. *J. of Social Issues,* 1968, 24, 103–111.

Kahn, R. L.: Productivity and Job Satisfaction. *Personnel Psychology,* 1960, 13, 275–287.

Kahn, D. M., R. P. Quinn, and J. D. Snoek: *Organizational Stress.* New York, John Wiley, 1964.

Klein, M.: Our Adult World and Its Roots in Infancy. *Tavistock Pamphlet,* no. 2, 1959.

Kornhauser, A.: *Mental Health of the Industrial worker: A Detroit Study.* New York, John Wiley, 1965.

Kuhn, T. S.: *The Structure of Scientific Revolutions.* Chicago, University of Chicago Press, 1962.

Langer, W. C.: *Psychology and Human Living.* New York, Appleton-Century-Crofts, 1937.

Lawler, E. E., and L. W. Porter: Perceptions Regarding Management Compensation. *Industrial Relations,* 1963, 3, 41–49.

Lawson, R. and M. H. Marx: Frustration: Theory and Experiment. *Genetic Psychology Monographs,* 1958, 57, 393–464.

Lesieur, F. G. (Ed.): *The Scanlon Plan.* Cambridge, Mass., M.I.T. Press, 1959.

Lewin, K.: *Field Theory in Social Science.* New York, Harper and Row, 1951.

Lindzey, G.: The Assessment of Human Motives. In Lindzey, G. (Ed.): *Assessment of Human Motives.* New York, Holt, Rinehart, and Winston, 1958, pp. 3–32.

Locke, E. A.: What is Job Satisfaction? *Organizational Behavior and Human Performance*, 1969, 4, 309–336.

McClelland, D. C., J. W. Atkinson, R. A. Clark, and E. L. Lowell: *The Achievement Motive*. New York, Appleton-Century-Crofts, 1953.

McGregor, D.: *The Human Side of Enterprise*. New York, McGraw-Hill, 1960.

Maslow, A. H.: A Theory of Human Motivation. *Psychological Review*, 1943, 50, 370–396.

Maslow, A. H.: *Eupsychian Management: A Journal*. Homewood, Ill., Irwin-Dorsey, 1965.

Maslow, A. H.: *Motivation and Personality*. New York, Harper, 1954.

Maslow, A. H.: *Toward a Psychology of Being*. Princeton, N.J., D. Van Nostrand, 1962.

Montgomery, M. R. and J. A. Monkman: The Relations between Fear and Exploratory Behavior. *J. of Comparative and Physiological Psychology*, 1955, 48, 132–136.

Montgomery, K. C.: The Role of Exploratory Drive in Learning. *J. of Comparative and Physiological Psychology*, 1954, 49, 60–64.

Morse, N. C.: *Satisfactions in the White Collar Job*. Ann Arbor, Survey Research Center, University of Michigan 1953.

Moskos, C. C.: Why Men Fight. *Transaction*, 1969, 7, 13–23.

Murray, E. J.: *Motivation and Emotion*. Englewood Cliffs, N. J., Prentice-Hall, 1964.

Murray, H. A.: *Explorations in Personality*. New York, Oxford Press, 1938.

Nealey, S. M.: Pay and Benefit Preference. *Industrial Relations*, 1963, 3, 17–28.

Newcomb, T. M.: *Stabilities Underlying Changes in Interpersonal Attraction*. *J. of Abnormal and Social Psychology*, 1963, 66, 376–386.

Newman, C. W.: The Influence of Dissatisfaction upon what Workers Want in their Jobs. Unpublished master's thesis, Stanford University, 1948.

Payne, R.: Factor Analysis of a Maslow-type Need Satisfaction Questionnaire. *Personnel Psychology*, 1970, 23, 251–268.

Porter, L. W.: Job Attitudes in Management: I. Perceived Deficiencies in Need Fulfillment as a Function of Job Level. *J. of Applied Psychology*, 1962, 46, 375–384.

Porter, L. W.: Job Attitudes in Management: II. Perceived Importance of Needs as a Function of Job Level. *J. of Applied Psychology*, 1963, 47, 141–148.

Porter, L. W. and E. E. Lawler: *Managerial Attitudes and Performance*. Homewood, Ill., Dorsey Press, 1968.

Porter, L. W.: *Organizational Patterns of Managerial Job Attitudes*. American Foundation for Management Research, 1964.

Rabkin, L. Y. and K. Rabkin: Children of the Kibbutz. *Psychology Today*, 1969, 3, 40–47.

Revans, R. W.: *Standards for Morale: Cause and Effect in Hospitals*. New York, Oxford Press, 1964.

Roach, D. E.: Dimensions of Employee Morale. *Personnel Psychology*, 1958, 11, 419–431.

Roberts, K. H., G. A. Walter, and R. E. Miles: A Factor-Analytic Study of Job Satisfaction Items Designed to Measure Maslow Need Categories. *Proceedings of the 78th Annual Convention of the American Psychological Association*, 1970, pp. 591–592.

Rogers, C.: *On Becoming a Person*. Boston, Houghton-Mifflin, 1961.

Rogers, C.: A Theory of Therapy, Personality, and Interpersonal Relationships as Developed in the Client-centered Framework. In Koch, S. (Ed.): *Psychology: A Study of a Science*, vol. III, *Formulations of the Person and the Social Context*. New York, McGraw-Hill, 1959, 184–256.

Rosenthal, R.: *Experimenter Effects in Behavioral Research*. New York, Appleton-Century-Crofts, 1966.

Rosenzweig, S.: An Outline of Frustration Theory. In Hunt, J. M. (Ed.): *Personality and the Behavior Disorders*. New York, Ronald Press, 1944, pp. 379–388.

Schein, E. H.: *Organizational Psychology*. Englewood Cliffs, N.J., Prentice-Hall, 1965.

Scott, W. E.: Activation Theory and Task Design. *Organizational Behavior and Human Performance*, 1966, 1, 3–30.

Seashore, S. and D. G. Bowers: *Changing the Structure and Functioning of an Organization*. Ann Arbor, Survey Research Center, University of Michigan, 1963.

Slater, C.: Some Factors Associated with Internalization of Motivation towards Occupational Role Performance. Unpublished doctoral dissertation, University of Michigan, 1959.

Storr, A.: *The Integrity of the Personality*. Baltimore, Penguin, 1960.

Strauss, G.: Some Notes on Power Equalization. In Leavitt, H.: *The Social Science of Organizations*. Englewood Cliffs, N.J., Prentice-Hall, 1963, pp. 41–84.

Strauss, G. and L. R. Sayles: *Personnel*. Englewood Cliffs, N.J., Prentice-Hall, 1967.

Sullivan, H. S.: *The Interpersonal Theory of Psychiatry*. New York, John Wiley, 1953.

Twery, R., J. Schmid, and C. Wrigley: Some Factors in Job Satisfaction: A Comparison of Three Methods of Analysis. *Educational and Psychological Measurement*, 1958, 18, 189–202.

Vroom, V. H.: A Comparison of Static and Dynamic Correlational Methods in the Study of Organizations. *Organizational Behavior and Human Performance*, 1966, 1, 55–70.

Vroom, V. H.: *Work and Motivation*. New York, John Wiley, 1964.

Walker, C. R. and R. H. Guest: *The Man on the Assembly Line*. Cambridge, Mass., Harvard University Press, 1952.

Walters, R. H.: The Effects of Social Isolation and Social Interaction on Learning and Performance in Social Situations. In Glass, D. C. (Ed.): *Environmental Influences*. New York, Russell Sage, 1968, pp. 155–184.

Walters, R. H. and R. D. Parke: Emotional Arousal, Isolation, and Discrimination Learning in Children. *J. of Experimental Child Psychology*, 1964, 1, 163–173.

Walters, R. H. and G. B. Henning: Social Isolation, Effect of Instructions, and Verbal Behavior. *Canadian Journal of Psychology*, 1962, 16, 202–210.

Wherry, R. J.: An Orthogonal Rerotation of the Baehr and Ash Studies of the S.R.A. Employee Inventory. *Personnel Psychology*, 1954, 7, 365–380.

Wherry, R. J.: Factor Analysis of Morale Data: Reliability and Validity. *Personnel Psychology*, 1958, 11, 78–89.

White, R. W.: Competence and the Psychosexual Stages of Development. *Nebraska Symposium on Motivation*, 1960, 97–141.

White, R. W.: Ego and Reality in Psychoanalytic Theory. *Psychological Issues*, III, monograph II, 1963.

White, R. W.: Motivation Reconsidered: The Concept of Competence. *The Psychological Review*, 1959, 66, 297–333.

Whyte, W. F.: *Organizational Behavior: Theory and Application.* Homewood, Ill., Dorsey, 1969.

Will, F. E. and D. C. King: A Factor Analytic Approach to the Construct and Content Validation of a Job Attitude Questionnaire. *Personnel Psychology*, 1965, 18, 81–90.

Wright, M. E.: Constructiveness of Play as Affected by Group Organization and Frustration. *Character and Personality*, 1942, 11, 40–49.

Wright, M. E.: The Influence of Frustration upon the Social Relations of Young Children. *Character and Personality*, 1943, 12, 111–122.

Zaleznik, A. and D. Moment: *The Dynamics of Interpersonal Behavior.* New York, John Wiley, 1964.

Zaleznik, A.: *Human Dilemmas of Leadership.* New York, Harper and Row, 1966.

Zaleznik, A.: Management of Disappointment. *Harvard Business Review*, 1967, 45, 59–70.

Zigler, E. and J. Williams: Institutionalization and the Effectiveness of Social Reinforcement: A Three year Follow-up Study. *J. of Abnormal and Social Psychology*, 1963, 66, 199–205.

Zigler, E., D. Balla, and E. C. Butterfield: A Longitudinal Investigation of the Relationship between Preinstitutional Social Deprivation and Social Motivation in Institutionalized Retardates. *J. of Personality and Social Psychology*, 1968, 10, 437–445.

INDEX

Ainsworth, M. S., 36
Allport, G. W., 9, 12
Andrews, F. M., 45
Appley, M. H., 41
Argyris, C., 5, 10, 50, 56, 57, 113
Assembly-line technique, effects of, 43, 46
Atkinson, J. W., 24
Attitudes
  behavior variables and, 96-100
  correlations between E.R.G. need
    satisfactions and other job
    related, 98, 99
  employee, 34, 39, 40
  managerial job, 42-43
  questionnaire on job, 167-74

Baer, D. M., 38
Balla, D., 38
Barker, R. G., 12, 42, 45
Barnes, L. B., 51
Baumgartel, H., 45
Beer, M., 51, 53-66
Behavior
  attitude and variables in, 96-100
  correlations between need
    satisfaction and Adolescent
    Lab observed, 100
Belongingness satisfaction, Maslow
  theory and, 28
Berkowitz, L., 21, 133
Bettelheim, B., 37
Bowers, D. G., 48
Bowlby, J., 36-38
Brown, D., 59
Brozek, J., 32
Butterfield, E. C., 38

Campbell, D. T., 71
Campbell, J. P., 7
Causality, 150-51
Challenge, 41, 42
Children
  constructiveness in play and
    friendship among, 45
  frustration-regression experiments
    with, 42
  growth frustration and relatedness
    desires of, 46-47
  maternal deprivation and, 36-38
  mutuality and, 39
Chronic desire scales, E.R.G., 82-83
Chronic desires
  defined, 8
  field settings for, 60
  measures of, 68-69, 168
  relating to satisfaction, 28
  relation between satisfaction and, 18
Chronic existence needs, studies
  of, 50
Chronic growth desires, growth
  satisfaction and, 140-42
Chronic relatedness desires,
  relatedness satisfaction and, 127-30
Clark, J. B., 51
Cofer, C. N., 41
Comparative utility, 154
Competence motivation, 132
Conant, J. B., 154
Congruence, 45
Content theories (substantive
  theories), 7
Convergent validity, 71-88, 156